Alex Crawford

Shipbuster
Mosquito Mk XVIII "Tse-tse"
An operational history

STRATUS

Table of contents

Published in Poland in 2008
by STRATUS s.c.
Po. Box 123,
27-600 Sandomierz 1, Poland
e-mail: office@mmpbooks.biz
for
Mushroom Model Publications,
36 Ver Road, Redbourn,
AL3 7PE, UK.
e-mail: rogerw@mmpbooks.biz
© 2008 Mushroom Model
Publications.
http://www.mmpbooks.biz

ISBN
978-83-89450-45-6

Editor in chief
Roger Wallsgrove

Editorial Team
Bartłomiej Belcarz
Robert Pęczkowski
Artur Juszczak
James Kightly

Scale Plans
Dariusz Karnas

Colour Drawings
Teodor Liviu Morusanu

DTP
Artur Bukowski

Printed by
Drukarnia Diecezjalna,
ul. Żeromskiego 4,
27-600 Sandomierz
tel. +48 (15) 832 31 92;
fax +48 (15) 832 77 87
www.wds.pl
marketing@wds.pl

PRINTED IN POLAND

Introduction

The two Mosquitos skimmed across the wave-tops at less than 100ft in order to avoid radar contact. Visibility to the horizon, at this altitude, was about 8 miles. The leader spotted the low silhouette of a U-boat's conning tower. After alerting his wingman the two aircraft pulled up into a climb. At 1,500ft they levelled off and prepared for the attack. Down below the U-boat, now fully alert and with guns manned, prepared for the onslaught. The leader called out, 'Attack attack attack' and both Mosquitos lined up on the U-boat. The gunners opened up and almost immediately they saw one of the aircraft enveloped in flames. Their shouts of joy gave way to dismay as the Mosquito continued on, emitting gouts of flame almost every second. The sea around the U-boat boiled with explosions that were far too large to be 20mm cannon shells. The U-boat staggered under the impact of two hits and the Captain ordered his men below and crash-dived to safety. In the control room the Captain wondered what new weapon had been fired at his boat. Damage control reported a number of small leaks but nothing important had been damaged.

The 'Wooden Wonder', 'Balsa Bomber', call it what you will, the de Havilland DH98 Mosquito was perhaps the world's first multi-role combat aircraft. Designed initially as a high speed unarmed bomber it was later to be developed into a highly successful fighter-bomber and night-fighter. One of the more interesting versions was the MkXVIII. This version was originally designed as a replacement for the Hurricane IID and was to be armed with a 6pdr (57mm) Molins gun. Only 17 Mosquitos, plus one prototype, were equipped with the Molins gun, but what they lacked in numbers they sure made up for it in the damage they caused the *Kriegsmarine*. Operating in ones and twos they scoured the Bay of Biscay and later the fjords of Norway looking for the elusive U-boats, their main prey. Later they carried out attacks on enemy shipping as well. The pilots of these aircraft braved the intense flak that the vessels threw up at them. With only time for one or two passes they had to make each shot count. A couple of well-placed shots would certainly disable a U-boat if not sink it.

The aircraft were operated by 618 Squadron Special Detachment and 248 Squadron from Predannack and Portreath in Cornwall, and Banff in Scotland, finally ending up with 254 Squadron at North Coates on the south east coast. After the war the survivors lingered on for a while in various Maintenance Units until they were struck off charge and scrapped by 1946-47.

So read on. I hope you enjoy this small chapter in the Mosquito's glorious career.

Molins 6 pdr gun

Specification	
Bore:	57mm (2.25in)
Action:	Recoil
Cyclic rate:	60rpm
Weight of shell:	7.1lb (3.2kg)
Weight of gun:	1,800lb (816kg)
Muzzle velocity:	2,600ft/sec (762m/sec)
Ammunition feed:	Molins automatic feed
Magazine capacity:	24 (23 in the magazines and 1 in the breech)
Sighting:	Dual graticule MkIIIa reflector sight
Length:	12ft 5in (3.8m)

The Molins gun was basically a development of the 6pdr anti-tank gun, as fitted to a number of British Army tanks, such as the Crusader III, Centaur I, Cromwell I-III and Churchill III, IV and X. The gun was also used by the United States Army, designated 57mm M1. In order to provide the Army with a fast moving, rapid firing anti-tank gun, it was decided to fit an automatic loader to the 6pdr. These rapid firing guns could then be mounted on the back of trucks or similar light vehicles and provide the advancing troops with an effective anti-tank weapon. The Molins Machinery Company was charged with designing and producing a suitable automatic loader system. The Molins Company were well known for their cigarette making machinery. In February 1942 work commenced on a suitable autoloader under the direction of Desmond Molins. Felix Ruau, a Frenchman, aided him. A hopper was designed to be fitted to the right hand side of the gun. On this hopper were five racks or magazines that held a total of 23 rounds of ammunition in groups of 5,

A drawing showing the general layout of the Molins gun and ammunition feed assembly.

(Andy Bird)

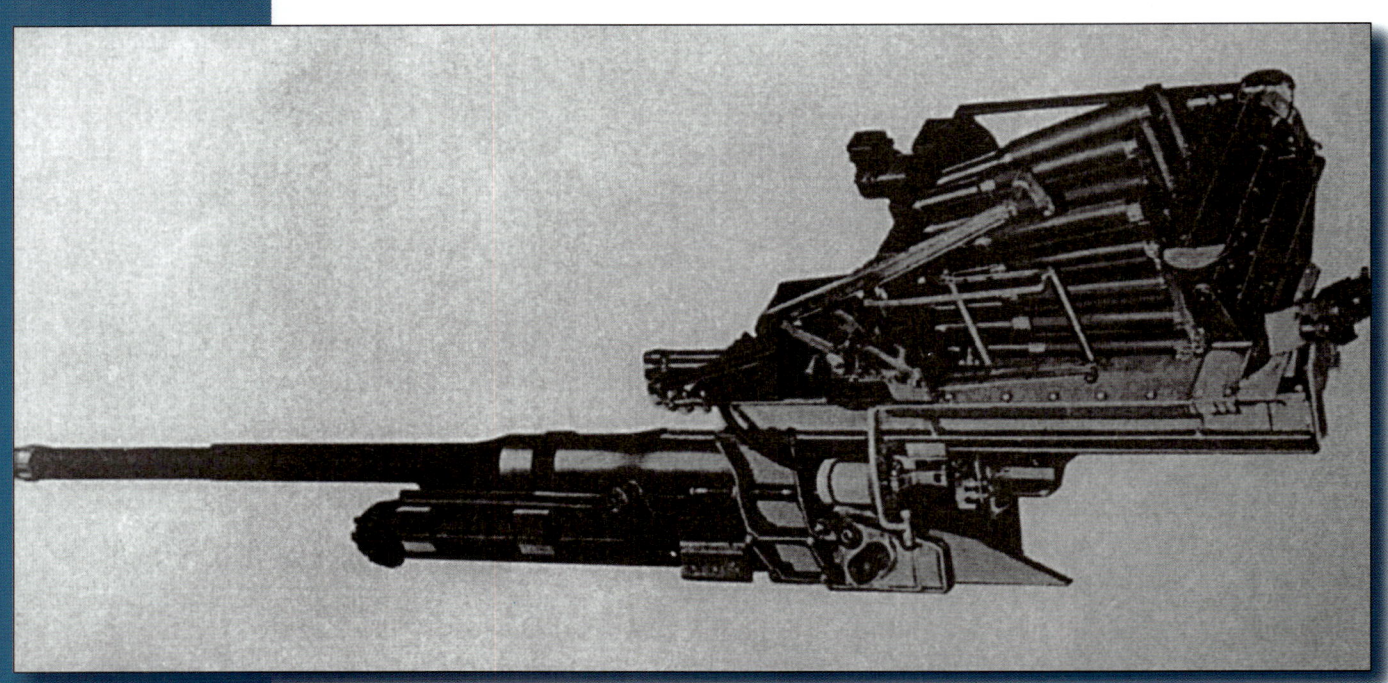

4, 5, 4 and 5. As one group was fired the next group of rounds was moved towards the breech by an electrical worm gear. The empty racks were moved to the left of the gun. As with all new inventions a number of modifications were carried out. This gun, now known as the Molins gun, was ready by August 1942 when it was taken to the nearby Deptford Shooting Club firing range. After a number of firings it was taken to Woolwich for exhaustive tests. By the time the trails had been completed the project had been cancelled, as the 6pdr was no longer deemed to be powerful enough to penetrate the latest German tanks, especially the Tiger tank which had just entered service.

The Royal Navy then became interested in the 6pdr, as they were looking for a quick firing, heavy calibre weapon to fit to their MTBs. Their autoloader held six rounds with one up the breach. Another twelve rounds were held in a ready to use rack on the mounting. This version was semi-automatic with the gunner having to fire each round individually. This version of the gun was known as the 6pdr QF Mk IIA, with over 600 being used on RN Vessels.

The RAF had a successful tank buster in the form of the Hurricane IID, but were looking to replace this with something more powerful. Discussions took place in early 1943 about a successor to the Hurricane IID. The question of using the Molins gun was brought up, and after some discussion the Air Staff asked the RAF gun section to trial the Molins gun for suitability in an aircraft. A number of ground firing tests were carried under the guidance of Mr G F Wallace. The trials were successful, although questions were raised about the gun's ability to operate under flying conditions. De Havilland was approached about the possibility of fitting the 6pdr to a Mosquito. As de Havilland had already carried out a feasibility study on fitting a 3.7inch anti-aircraft gun to the Mosquito, they readily agreed to give the smaller Molins gun a try. An experimental unit was set up at Hatfield to work on this new project. Although known as the Molins gun, the technical name for this weapon was the "QF 6pdr Class M Mark I with Auto Loader Mk III."

The front end of a crashed Mosquito FBVI was used to work out how the gun would be fitted and how the blast would effect the airframe. As the gun would be inaccessible once installed in the aircraft the gun was to be armed and ready to fire before the aircraft left the ground. This meant that there would be one round in the breach primed and ready to fire. Work commenced quickly and by 29th April 1943 the mock-up was placed in the butts at Hatfield and loaded with five rounds. Firing trials were also carried out under the eyes of the ever-watchful Ministry of Aircraft Production (MAP). After the firing test it was found that a fixing bolt had sheared and so two days later the gun was installed into another FBVI fuselage to find out the best way to fit the auto feed unit and gun. It was found necessary to offset the gun 4 inches to starboard of the aircraft's centre line. The MAP agreed that the idea seemed to be feasible and an order was placed for

Two views of a naval 6pdr as fitted to the bows of a Motor Gun Boat (MGB). The ammunition rack only held 6 rounds with reloads being held in a ready rack next to the gun. The gun could be fired either manually or semi-automatic.

(IWM negatives A25162 and A25164)

a prototype aircraft to be fully installed with the Molins gun. With the installation complete a brand new FBVI, HJ732, was wheeled into Hatfield's experimental bay for conversion into the MkXVIII prototype.

The differences between the FB VI and Mk XVIII were slight. The wing structure at the centre wing rib was modified and the two centre fuel tanks were omitted. Inside the fuselage the No2 bulkhead was modified to accept the gun barrel passing through it. The gun bay doors were also modified. The engines and the fuselage in the region of the cockpit were armour plated, as was part of the starboard gun bay door that covered the gun breech and magazine.

Due to the weight of the Molins gun and the additional armour the Mk XVIII was a very heavy aircraft, and it was therefore desirable to have maximum power at take-off. As such it was powered by two Merlin 25 engines. These were fitted with a specially adapted and adjusted supercharger, and generated 1,640 hp at 2,000ft.

Wing drop tanks were fitted as standard and an extra fuel tank was placed in the rear of the gun bay. Some aircraft may have been 'wired' for rocket projectiles and bombs but these were never used by the Mk XVIII, as due to the long range of their missions the drop tanks were a necessity. As the aircraft was originally designed as a tank buster, to operate in North Africa, provision was made for the installation of desert equipment. As we shall see the role of the aircraft changed and this equipment was never used.

GUN INSTALLATION

The Molins 57mm gun is mounted in the gun bay in place of the four 20mm cannon. The axis of the piece was mounted offset to starboard by 4inch to the aircraft's centre line and parallel to the fore and aft line of the aircraft and is depressed $3\frac{1}{4}°$ down from the rigging datum. The muzzle protrudes some 2ft from the nose. The 'G' load of the gun is taken direct to the centre section of the main spar. The side loads are taken by two struts, one of which is picked up by the port extremity of the armour plating beneath the pilot's cockpit. The other strut goes to the starboard side of the fuselage towards the rear of the gun bay. The main recoil force is taken up by other struts, which are fitted to the horizontal plating beneath the pilot's cockpit. The rear of the gun and feed mechanism is supported by a strong point attached to the roof in the rear of the gun bay.

The gun can be raised into position and lowered to the ground by a 4,000lb capacity bomb winch installed in the roof of the gun bay. Access to the gun bay is by means of the two bomb bay doors. The starboard door was wider than the port door due to the ejection chute being fitted. Forward of the gun bay doors is a removable panel, which allows the gun to be removed and installed. This panel has a blister to the rear of it, which continues on to the starboard gun bay door, which provides clearance for the buffer. A metal blast cover protects the nose of the aircraft.

MAINTENANCE

The oil level in the buffer was checked either weekly or after every 50 rounds have been fired, whichever occurs first. This was due to a continued seepage from the buffer cylinder. The recoil slides were greased at every aircraft inspection. The breech block and breech ring was wiped over with an oily cloth every day. After every time the gun was fired the barrel was run through with a lightly oiled cleaning brush. After every 160 rounds that have been fired the barrel was gauged for wear.

The feed mechanism was inspected daily and all worm drives and shafts of the automatic changeover mechanism had anti-freeze grease applied. All other bare metal parts of the gun were inspected and wiped down with an oily cloth on a daily basis.

The metal plate with the hole in it is the front lifting bracket. This is where the winch was attached to hoist the gun into the bomb bay. At the bottom of the picture can be seen the two forward mounting arms.

(Roger Wallsgrove)

The ammunition hopper held five 'chargers'. Each of these 'chargers' had a 'base guide' and a 'nose guide', which could hold up to five rounds of 6pdr shells. The usual load was 5-4-5-4-5.

(Alex Crawford)

The 'depressor arm' would normally sit on top of uppermost round. This would apply pressure on the rounds and so feed them down into the breech.

(Roger Wallsgrove)

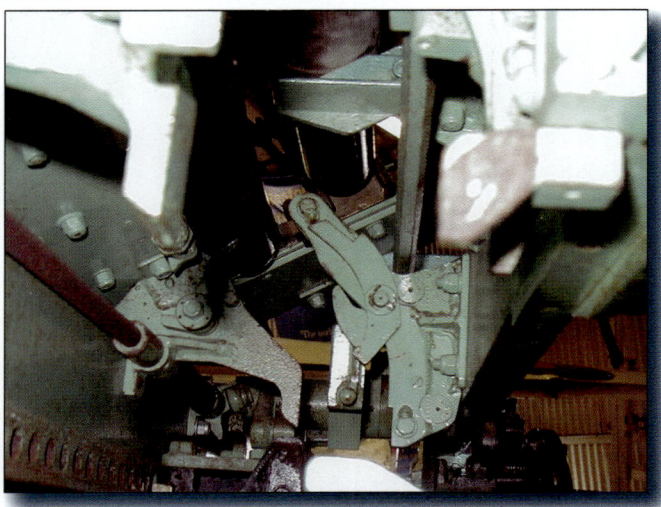

As the 'charger' reached the 'discharge position' the nose of the round would drop down the chute and into the breach. The arm would then engage the rear of the round and ram it home. The breach would close and the round would be ready to fire.

(Roger Wallsgrove & Alex Crawford)

As the last round was fired a worm gear would be activated and the empty 'charger' would be moved to the left of the hopper. A new 'charger' would be moved to the 'discharge position' and the next round rammed home.

(Roger Wallsgrove)

The business end of the Molins 6pdr. This view also shows that the ammunition hopper sits at an angle.

(Roger Wallsgrove)

The force of the recoil is taken up by the oil filled buffer, which sits below the gun barrel. When the buffer was filled to the correct level the recoil forces measured out at 6,400lb.

(Roger Wallsgrove & Alex Crawford)

On either side of the gun barrel were the two front mounting arms. These were attached to the gun front mountings, diagonal struts and port and starboard steady struts.

(Roger Wallsgrove)

9

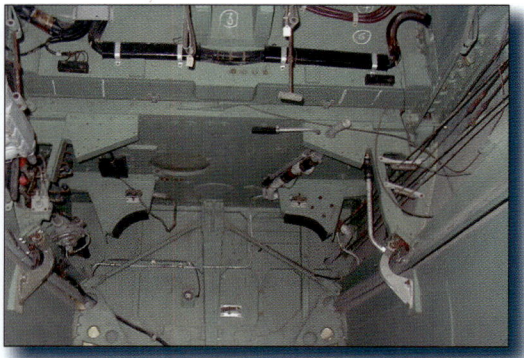

An extra fuel tank was fitted to the rear of the gunbay. The No2 bulkhead as fitted for the 4 x 20mm cannon. It was suitably modified to accept the larger bore of the 6pdr. The exposed control wires and fuel pipes were covered over to prevent them from being snagged by the 6pdr and auto-feed assembly.

These photos are of an FB.Mk VI, the a/c under restoration at the de Havilland Aircraft Museum in Hertfordshire, UK.

(Alex Crawford)

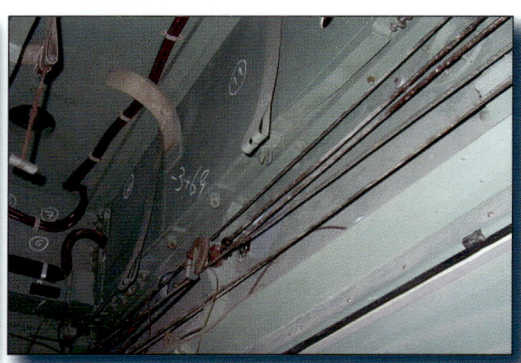

Four general views of the ammunition hopper.
(Roger Wallsgrove).

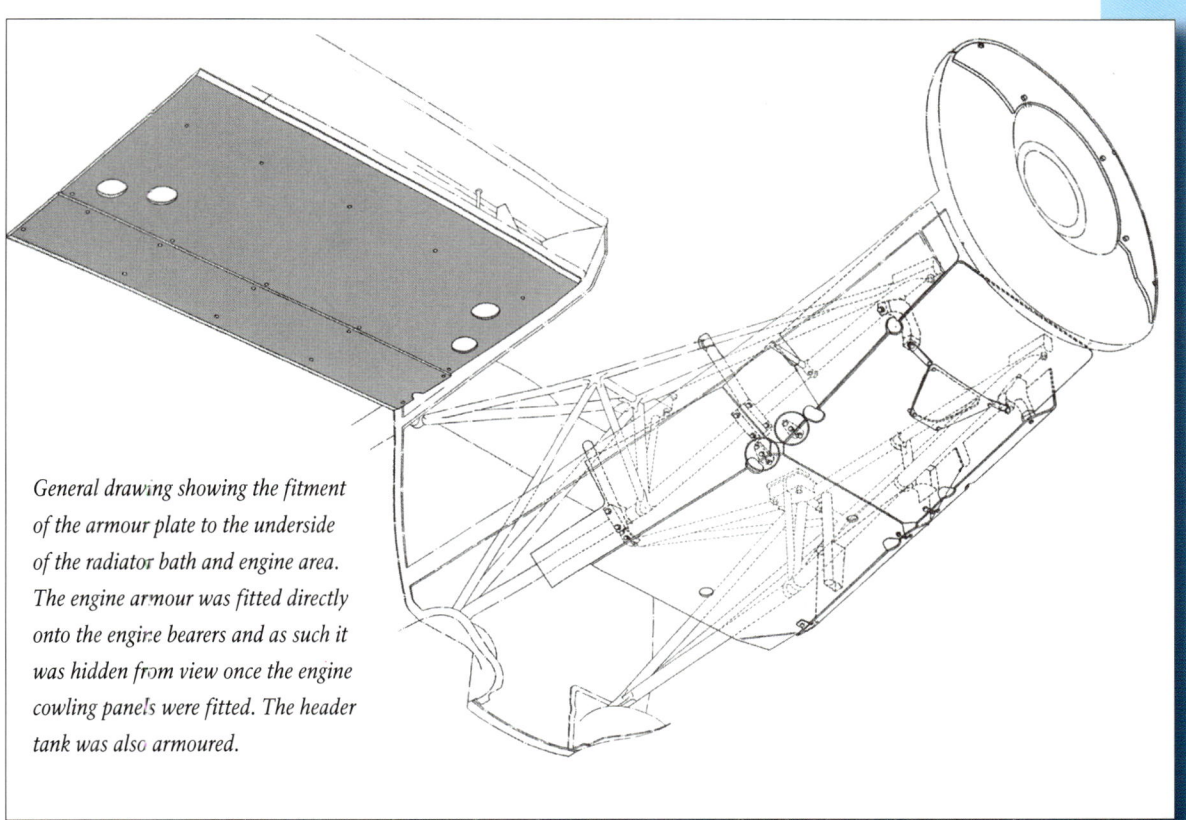

General drawing showing the fitment of the armour plate to the underside of the radiator bath and engine area. The engine armour was fitted directly onto the engine bearers and as such it was hidden from view once the engine cowling panels were fitted. The header tank was also armoured.

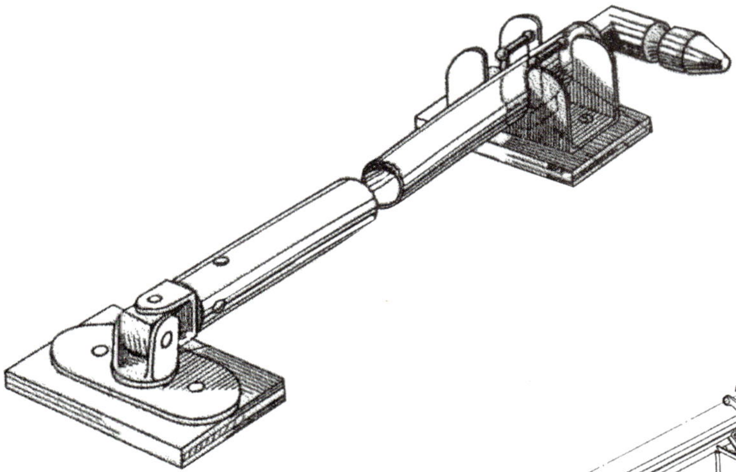

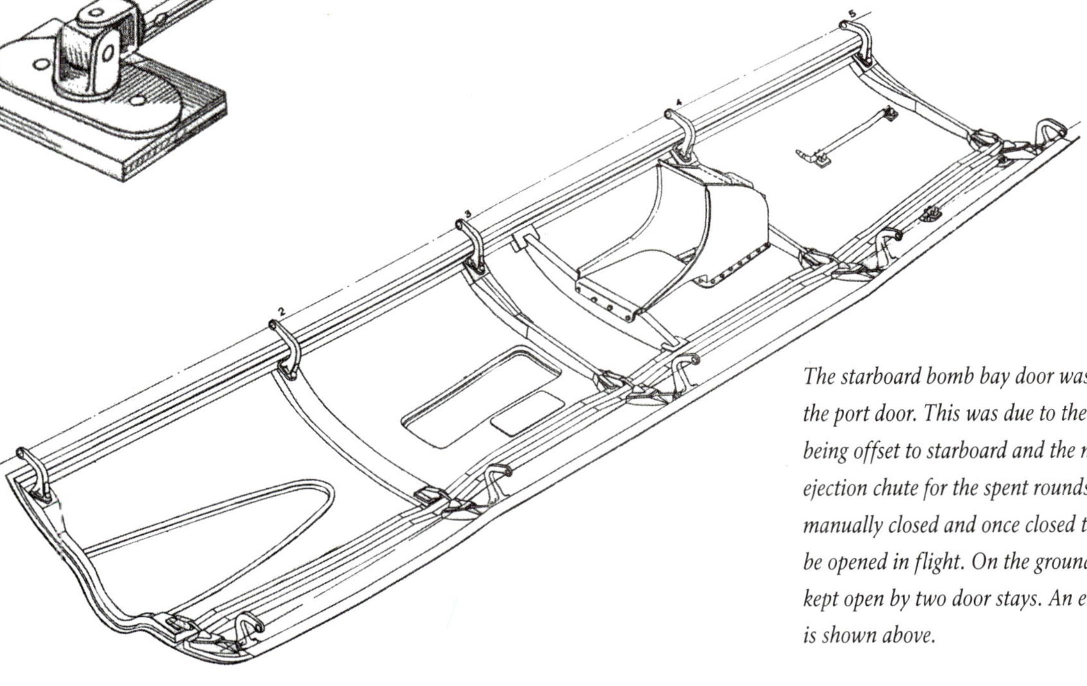

The starboard bomb bay door was wider than the port door. This was due to the Molins gun being offset to starboard and the need to fit an ejection chute for the spent rounds. The doors were manually closed and once closed they could not be opened in flight. On the ground the doors were kept open by two door stays. An enlarged drawing is shown above.

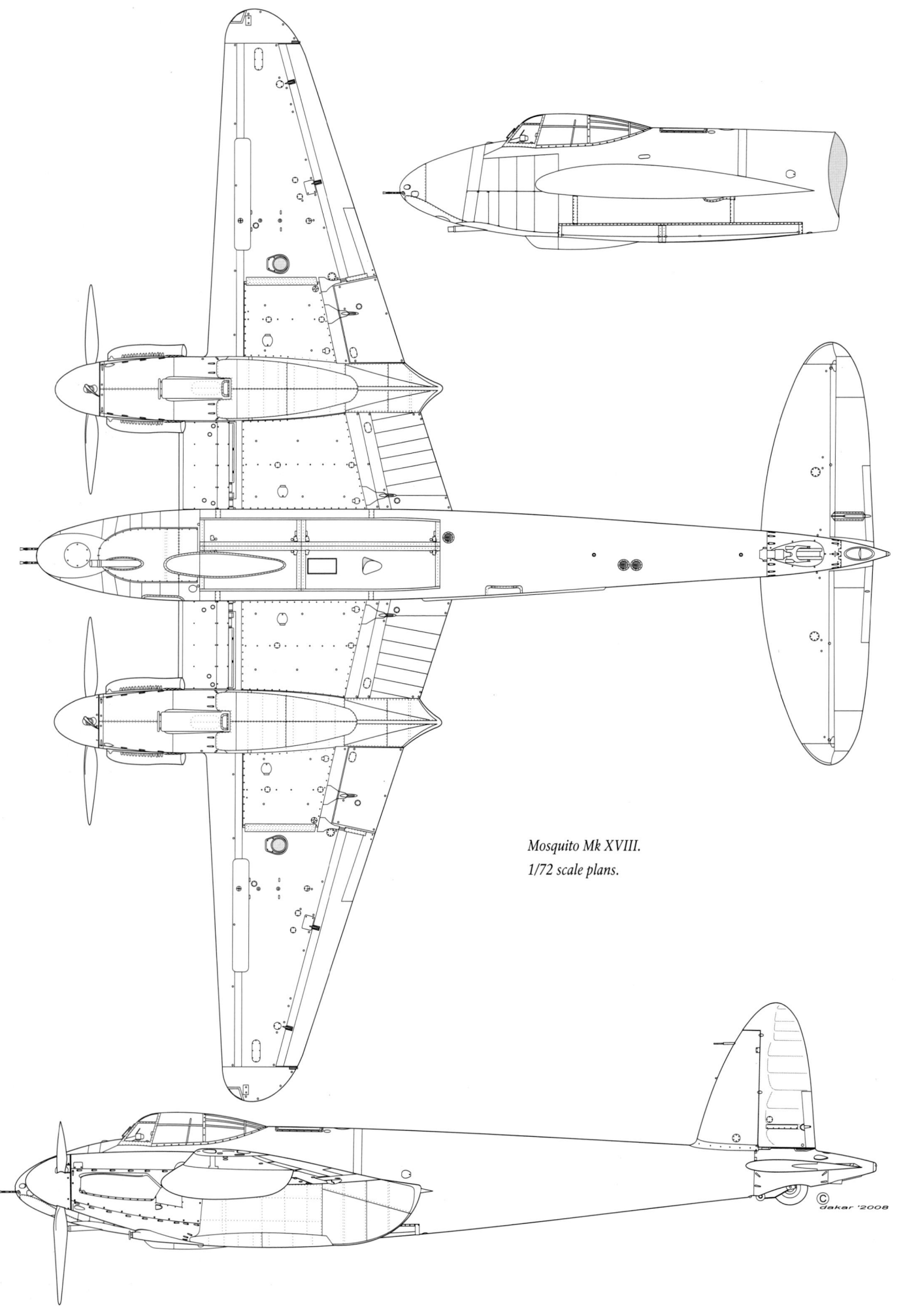

Mosquito Mk XVIII.
1/72 scale plans.

dakar '2008

GROUND TRIALS

Ground firing trials took place at the Aircraft & Armament Experimental Establishment (A&AEE) at Boscombe Down between 12th June and 1st July 1943. Mosquito Mk XVIII prototype HJ732 took part in all the trials. Representatives from Molins and de Havilland were present during the trials to provide any technical advice and assistance as and when required. These trials showed up a number of faults in the installation and feed system of the gun.

During firing trials with APC ammunition a total of 21 stoppages occurred where the rounds failed to feed into the breech. It was found that the nose of the round failed to drop into the ramming position. There was insufficient downward pressure on the magazine arm to force the nose of the round down. Molins carried out some modifications to the magazine arm to ensure the rounds would be forced down into position. After this modification was made 45 rounds were fired without any further stoppages of this kind.

Below the barrel of the gun is the recoil buffer. This oil-filled buffer absorbed the tremendous recoil of the gun. The recoil takes place in approximately 0.24 seconds and the run out is approximately 0.74 seconds. The maximum point of the recoil is at 0.4 seconds. When the gun was first fired it was done so without checking the buffer oil level. As a result the recoil force was measured at 9,300lb. When the buffer was filled to the correct level the forces measured out at 6,400lb. If the buffer was not filled to the correct level then the excessive forces applied during recoil could cause damage to the gun mounting points, and at worst knock the gun loose during flight with dire consequences for the crew.

Careful observation of blast and shock damage throughout the trials was maintained. Some minor damage was noted and recommendations were put in place to strengthen these areas.

> Rivets in the engine nacelle panel stiffening ribs sheared, causing the panels to bow so that the radiator temperature control flaps fouled the distorted panels.
> Exhaust manifold screws worked loose.
> Dzus fasteners on the engine cowls became strained.
> The VHF set was switched off.
> Gun bay door catches became strained and stretched.
> The inner flaps lost their covering after firing over 500 rounds.

A chute for the ejection of the empty shell cases was fitted to the starboard gun bay door. When the gun reached its maximum recoil the empty case was ejected backwards towards the chute. It was assessed that the empty cases would fall 3-4ft clear of the tail. Some damage was inflicted to the chute by the recoil of the gun and by the empty cases themselves. This minor damage was not considered a problem.

The flash from normally filled ammunition was fine for normal ground operations, but not for air operations. In some instances the pilot, who sat in the aircraft to observe the trials, took up to 15 seconds to regain full vision. Flashless ammunition was

A ground crewman of 248 Squadron holds up a 6pdr shell for a publicity shot.

(Andy Bird)

recommended and the trials proved that there was very little flash from these shells and the pilot's vision was not impaired in any way.

Targets were set up at 100 and 350yds. Single shots were fired and after each shot the gun alignment was rechecked. A high degree of accuracy was obtained, although this was to be expected when firing from a static aircraft. The trials did show that the shell dropped more than the official figure quoted. It was noticed that there was a half second lag from firing the gun to the round actually being fired. An improved firing solenoid was fitted which cured the problem.

Other recommendations included the fitting of a rounds counter and protection of the control cables that ran through the gun bay.

AIR FIRING TRIALS

The air firing trials took place at the Brandy Head range near Exeter during July 1943. This range was chosen as it was on the coast and passes could be made to seaward. The targets consisted of a 20ft square canvas sheet placed in front of a 30ft mild steel target. On the centre of this sheet was painted a 10ft cross with arms 2ft wide. A smaller 19ft by 9ft target with a 5ft-diameter circle was also used.

Seventeen shoots were flown during these trials with the number of rounds fired per shoot varied from one to twenty-five. Approaches were made in level flight and shallow dives, while the speeds varied between an Indicated Air Speed (IAS) of 240, 280 and 300 mph. One major problem was that when the aircraft pulled more than +/- 2g the gun had a tendency to jam. As the rounds were feed into the breech the 'g' force would cause them to jam. The feed was modified in such a way as to push the nose of the round down when the breech was opened. Although this helped to improve the feed in did not eliminate jams. Throughout its service life the Molins gun would still be prone to jamming.

With a muzzle velocity of 2,600 foot per second it was anticipated that when the shell reached 500yards there would be a trajectory drop of 9ft. Therefore the gun was adjusted laterally so that the projection of the axis of the piece cut a point in the vertical plane of the aircraft's centre line at a range of 500yds. In layman's terms this meant that when the shell reached 500yds the trajectory was at 0ft and would only then start to drop off.

A GJ3 reflector sight replaced the standard GM2 sight. This gave direct reflection of the graticule from the windscreen. The 50mph graticule was considered adequate for stationary or moving targets. A cine camera was installed to film, and later analyse, the shots but due to the blast from the gun this didn't always work. A number of modifications were carried out but it was still unsatisfactory.

During firing the nose of the aircraft dipped slightly, but there was no lateral throw off when the gun was fired. Crosswinds tended to cause the shell groupings to veer down wind and were caused by the either drifting or crabbing with the wind.

Due to the weight of the gun and the armour plating around the engines an optimum IAS of 280mph was recommended. Speeds below this caused stability problems and the rudder control was not so good. Speeds above 280mph were difficult

A front three-quarter view of a Tse-tse, possibly NT224/E1.
(Andy Bird)

to reach and maintain. Optimum range was considered to be around about 1,300yds depending on weather conditions. With a speed of 280mph it was possible to fire one round every 150-200yds (1.1-1.5 seconds). So with an attack starting at 1,000yds and breaking away at 500yds four shells could be fired. Single aimed shots were recommended as continuous shots, although slightly faster, caused loss of aim and accuracy.

Attacks were to be carried out along the length of the target and at an angle of 20-35°. Firing at a lower angle would only cause the shell to bounce of the casing of the submarine, which had become the main intended target. The initial aiming point was to be the conning tower. When firing from the beam, pilots were instructed to aim for the waterline. When the shells entered the water the flight of the shell was curved by the water so that it ran parallel to the surface until it hit the hull of the target, thus inflicting an underwater hit, causing flooding to the target.

F/O 'Hilly' Hilliard and W/O Hoyle. This crew carried out over 60 operational missions on the Tse-tse.

(A H Hiliard)

The ejection chute functioned properly and no empty shell casings were recorded as having hit the tail plane. However the ejection chute was hit on numerous occasions by the recoil of the gun and although a number of modifications were carried out it was still considered a problem area. It is possible that some aircraft were not fitted with an ejection chute and that the empty shell casings were retained within the gunbay only to be emptied when the aircraft returned to base. In conversation with a couple of Tse-tse pilots one recalled that the empty casings were retained while the other thought they were ejected.

By the time the trials were completed the RAF had lost interest in gun-armed tank buster aircraft, and the fate of the MkXVIII hung in the balance. Its saviour was Coastal Command, who were looking for an anti-shipping weapon big enough to punch holes in U-Boats and (later on) merchant vessels. It was decided to carry out trials with the aircraft in the anti-shipping role. An order for 30 sets of the Tse-tse modification kits was placed with de Havilland.

A further three Mosquito Mk VIs, HX902-HX904, were taken from the production line, contract number 555/C.23, at Hatfield and converted into Mk XVIIIs. Some of the Tse-tse retained the four machine guns while others had two of them removed and the ammo capacity for the remaining two increased. Due to the demand for Mosquito FB VI aircraft the conversion of the Mk XVIIIs took second place, and as such there were large gaps between the delivery dates of the aircraft. These Mosquitos soon earned the nickname "Tse-tse", which was derived from the fact that a Tse-tse fly was the same size as a Mosquito but packed a bigger punch.

INTO SERVICE

With the decision to use the Molins-equipped Mosquitos on operations the Air Ministry looked for a suitable squadron. None of the existing Mosquito squadrons were trained for low level work, until someone remembered that 618 Squadron had trained in low level work for the High Ball operation. As a result they were chosen to trial the new weapon. Four crews and thirty-four ground crew were selected to form 618 Squadron Special Detachment. The Detachment would be attached to 248 Squadron, based at Predannack and equipped with Beaufighters, mainly for administration purposes, but it would retain its own identity should the personnel be required by 618 Squadron. As the Special Detachment and its aircraft were still classified as secret it was to remain apart from 248 Squadron regarding all maintenance.

Three aircraft were delivered to 618 Squadron between September and October 1943. 618 Squadron had been formed in mid 1943 for use with the Highball anti-shipping bomb. Basically this was a scaled down version of the famous bouncing bomb developed by

Barnes Wallis that was used to breach the Möhne and Eder dams in Germany. The initial target for these smaller bombs was the German Tirpitz, which was hiding in a Norwegian fjord. The squadron had trained for weeks in Scotland for this mission. Numerous inert Highballs had been dropped and the squadron was ready for the operation. Unfortunately the raid on the dams put paid to the attack on Tirpitz, as Germans increased the protection on the areas they considered a high risk. Tirpitz was one of them and the defences around her were strengthened. The four crews selected to form the Special Detachment were:

– S/Ldr C Rose and Sgt S Cowley
– F/O A H Hilliard and W/O J Hoyle
– F/O A Bonnett, RCAF and F/O A D McNicol
– F/O D J Turner and F/O D Curtis

The crews arrived at Predannack to find they were allocated a hanger at the far end of the airfield. In the hanger was the first of their aircraft, HX902/G, the 'G' signifying that the aircraft had to be guarded at all times. The other two Mosquitos, HX903 and HX904, would arrive a few days later. S/Ldr Rose had spent some time at de Havilland and had carried out a number of flights in the Tse-tse prototype HJ732, so he was able to pass on some of his knowledge to the other crews. Training was very basic, as F/O Hilliard recalls:

"Training for the rest of the three crews at Predannack where the Detachment was formed was minimal. We were taken up and shown what happens, from thereon we practised at sea two or three times and that was that. We were confident and proved so on our missions."

The Special Detachment's main duty was coastal patrols and anti-shipping strikes in the Bay of Biscay, with their prime target being U-Boats going to and from their bases in Western France. The relatively shallow waters around the ports of Bordeaux, Brest, La Rochelle, Lorient and St Nazaire prevented the U-boats from diving when they were attacked. It was hoped that the U-boats would be prevented from using these waters if enough of them were sunk or badly damaged.

The future of the Tse-tse Mosquitos now lay in the results of these operational trials. In order to assess these results at least four successful attacks on U-Boats were required. With the capture of the Enigma coding machine Coastal Command HQ had the advantage of being able to track most of the U-boats in and around the Bay of Biscay area. As such they had a good idea of where to send the Mosquito crews and as a result it wasn't long before the Tse-tse were in action.

A 6pdr QF MkIIA or Molins guns mounted on an army 6pdr carriage sits next to a 248 Squadron Tse-tse at Portreath, Cornwall. This picture clearly demonstrates the size of the Molins gun and how difficult the task was to squeeze it into the bomb bay of a Mosquito.

(IWM negative CH18219)

Area of operations

The Bay of Biscay was divided into 7 patrols lines and covered the known channels that the U-boats used while entering and leaving port. The patrol lines were;

A	46°32'N 04°25'W	along a bearing of 360° true to the coast
B	46°32'N 04°52'W	along a bearing of 039° true to the coast
C	46°15'N 03°17'W	along a bearing of 030° true to the coast
D	45°40'N 03°07'W	along a bearing of 061° true to the coast
E	45°27'N 03°00'W	along a bearing of 078° true to the coast
F	45°02'N 02°29'W	along a bearing of 049° true to the coast
G	44°33'N 02°19'W	along a bearing of 029° true to the coast

The Squadron would receive a telephone call to indicate which patrol line was to be flown the next day. It was also advised that these calls could be received at short notice. Therefore the Squadron had to have a least one Tse-tse on one hour's readiness, with any other aircraft made available if they could be prepared for take-off within the allotted time.

The first Tse-tse mission took place on the morning of the 24th October. Two aircraft, HX902/O (S/Ldr Rose/Sgt Cowley) and HX904/E (F/O Hilliard and W/O Hoyle) carried out a sweep along the Bay of Biscay. After a fruitless search the aircraft returned to base. Although no enemy vessels were encountered it gave the pilots an idea as to how the Mosquito would handle with the weight of the big gun.

NOVEMBER

Two Tse-tse took off from Predannack airfield in Cornwall on the morning of 4th November. Their mission was to fly to the Bay of Biscay to look for and attack any U-Boats they saw. The aircraft were HX902/O (S/Ldr Rose/Sgt Cowley) and HX903/I (F/O Turner/F/O Curtis). After flying for some time along the French coast at 50 feet in order to avoid enemy radar, they reached their allocated search area. Both aircraft climbed to 3,000ft. There was no sign of any U-boats; all they could see was a solitary trawler. S/Ldr Rose dived down to investigate the lone vessel. It was assumed the trawler was a lookout post for submerged U-boats.

S/Ldr Rose ordered F/O Turner to orbit while he went down to attack the trawler. Rose fired off a number of shells, which hit the trawler and the boiler appeared to explode. Accurate return fire from the trawler hit Rose's Mosquito and the aircraft, trailing smoke, continued on its dive and crashed into the sea killing both occupants. The other Tse-tse returned to base.

On the 7th HX903/I (F/O Bonnet, RCAF/F/O McNicol) was on patrol over Channel B in the Bay of Biscay. Arriving at the designated point he climbed to 300ft to get a better view and almost immediately he spotted a U-boat on the surface. This boat, *U-123,*

Underside view of NT225 showing the under wing fuel tanks, landing lights and bomb bay doors.
(Paul Taylor)

Tse-Tse NT225/O with full D-Day markings somewhere over Southern England. The upper camouflage pattern can be clearly seen.

(Paul Taylor)

a Type IXB from 2 Flotille commanded by Oblt Horst von Schroeter, was returning to Brest from its 13th patrol. Bonnett climbed up to 1,500ft and turned to get the sun behind him. He then dived in to attack firing off 7 rounds in his first pass. A number of strikes were seen on the fore deck near the deck gun and aft of the conning tower. Dirty coloured smoke was also seen coming from the submarine. Coming round for a second attack his aircraft was hit by some of the accurate flak coming from the U-boat. To his dismay the Molins gun jammed, all he could do was to carry out a strafing run with his machine guns. During these two attacks *Bootsmannsmaat* Struve was killed and *Matrosenobergefreiter's* Fröbel and Noack wounded.

Bonnett returned to base and landed shortly after 11.30hrs. After this attack all submarines received an escort when travelling on the surface to and from port.

S/Ldr A D Philips, DFC and F/O R W Thomson arrived as replacements for S/Ldr Rose and F/Sgt Cowley on the 9th. Their time in the Special Detachment was short lived as they were transferred to 248 Squadron two weeks later. S/Ldr Philips and his navigator returned to the Detachment in early 1944.

On the 11th the two remaining Tse-tse, HX903/I (F/O Turner/F/O Curtis) and HX904/E (F/O Hilliard/F/Sgt Hoyle) took off to carry out a patrol off the French coast at 0700hrs. A number of trawlers were seen but not attacked. At 0908hrs a seagull collided with F/O Turner's Tse-tse. Damaged was caused to one of the spinners and the aircraft returned to base on one engine.

On the 16th two Tse-tse HX903/I (F/O Hilliard/F/Sgt Hoyle) and HX904/E (F/O Turner/F/O Curtis) were ordered out into the Western Approaches to find a LCT. The vessel had been part of a convoy and had been abandoned in rough seas. After a square search of the area the LCT was duly found. Both pilots carried out several attacks and fired off all their ammunition into the vessel. The LCT was still afloat when both pilots set course for base.

The rest of the month was pretty quiet for the Tse-tse crews, with very little operational flying. During November two further Mosquito Mk VIs, MM424 and MM425, were converted into Tse-tse. Also during the month of November 248 Squadron started to re-equip with Mosquito FB Mk VIs.

DECEMBER

A decision had been made to convert 248 Squadron from Beaufighters to Mosquitos. As such at the start of December two Mosquito Mk II and one Mosquito Mk III aircraft were allotted to 238 Squadron to assist in the conversion. The Tse-tse only carried out 7 sorties during the month. Poor weather conditions curtailed a lot of flying. The conversion to Mosquitos by 248 Squadron continued, but they still carried out numerous anti-shipping strikes with their remaining Beaufighters.

JANUARY 1944

The first month of the New Year would prove to be a quiet period for the squadron. Conversion to Mosquitos was a continuous programme and the last operational patrol to be carried out by the Beaufighters occurred on the 9th. The Beaufighter pilots required about one and a half-hours on dual before going solo on the Mosquito. Ground crews also received training in maintaining the airframe and engines. Adverse weather conditions also interrupted the flying training programme. By the end of January the pilots had received 29 hours on dual instruction and 32 hours on solo flying. Of the Beaufighters, there was only one left on squadron strength.

The Tse-tse crews carried out several patrols and although a number of enemy vessels were spotted none were attacked. During these patrols an increased number of fishing vessels were encountered. These vessels were usually stationary and on one occasion a large area of very calm bright green water was spotted. This was on the 7th when S/Ldr Phillips in a Mosquito Mk II, DK700, was escorting one of the Tse-tse, HX903/I (F/O Turner/ F/O Curtis), on a patrol over the Bay of Biscay. Near a stationary trawler they saw a large number of bubbles rising to the surface from a depth of 20-30 feet. After remaining in the area for some 20-25 minutes both aircraft departed for base. It was thought that these fishing vessels were somehow in touch with the submerged U-boats and kept them informed of any aircraft that were in the vicinity.

On the 14th HX903/I (F/O B C Roberts/F/Sgt P Winsor) was ordered out on patrol. F/O Hilliard and F/Sgt Hoyle in DK700 escorted the Tse-tse. Two enemy vessels of approximately 500-600t were observed. They had a high bow and a flush main deck with a break about one third of the way down the deck. A bridge superstructure with a mast on top and a short raked funnel completed the description. The aircraft turned to port and headed towards the vessels. The lead vessel fired off a number of cartridges, apparently six red and three green. The second vessel fired off the same number of cartridges and then the lead vessel opened fire with a light anti aircraft gun. The line of fire was accurate but the rounds fell short. With falling visibility the two Mosquitos avoided combat and headed back to base.

Poor weather curtailed further operations until the end of the month. Flying training on the Mk VI Mosquitos was also hampered by the weather. Only one and a half-hours had been flown over a period of eight days. On the 29th the Special Detachment carried out a patrol and sighted two merchant vessels as well as six trawlers and two smaller merchant vessels. No attacks were carried out and the aircraft returned to base.

F/O 'Hammy' Hamlett and his navigator W/O B Mudd joined the Special Detachment during January. The Detachment now had five crews and two Tse-tse, HX903/I and HX904/E, with the promised arrival of two more, MM424 and MM425. The Detachment also used a Mosquito Mk II, DK700/O, as well as the two Tse-tse during this period. From the available records it would appear that HX904 failed to partake in any operational flying during January. This may have been due to mechanical problems. With only one Tse-tse operational the Mk II would have given the five Special Detachment crews continued training and experience on type.

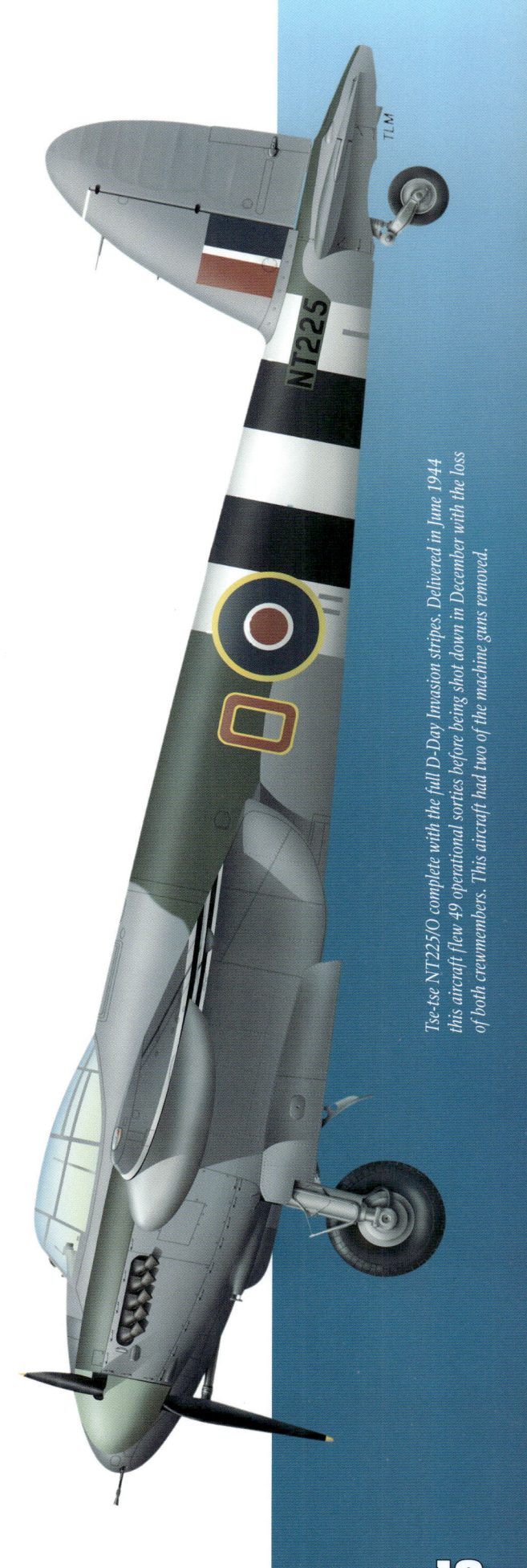

Tse-tse NT225/O complete with the full D-Day Invasion stripes. Delivered in June 1944 this aircraft flew 49 operational sorties before being shot down in December with the loss of both crewmembers. This aircraft had two of the machine guns removed.

Top and bottom views of the night fighter camouflage scheme applied to all Mosquito MkXVIII Tse-tse.

Portreath

FEBRUARY

Again poor weather hampered the flying training, although by the 3rd February 23 pilots had gone solo on the Mosquito. With the squadron being virtually non-operational due to the Mosquito conversion it was decided to move 248 Squadron from RAF Predannack to RAF Portreath, situated on the north coast of the Cornish Peninsula. These orders arrived on the 9th, and on the 14th an advance party of four NCOs and twenty-four airmen left for Portreath in order to prepare the living quarters, Flights and Sections for the arrival of the main party. All aircraft were flown to Portreath on the 16th. Four days later on the 20th the first operational sortie from Portreath was carried out. No Tse-tse operations were carried out during February, although training continued.

On the 26 February two more Tse-tse joined the squadron. They were MM424/H and MM425/L. Among the personnel who were posted into the squadron in February was S/Ldr O J M Barron, who was to take over command of the squadron with effect from 1st March.

MARCH

Two Tse-tse carried out a line patrol on the 4th and apart from spotting a large number of trawlers no other vessels were seen.

During the course of the Second World War a number of German and Japanese submarines carried vital war materials and exchanged information on weapons, engines and aircraft designs. One such Japanese submarine was *I-29*, which left Singapore for occupied France on 16 December 1943. The submarine, code named *Matsu* (Pine), was the fourth Japanese submarine to undertake this type of mission. She carried on board 16 passengers, Naval officers, engineers and specialists.

Allied code breakers had deciphered a signal that indicated *I-29's* final destination. Plans were put in motion to intercept the submarine in the Bay of Biscay. On 13 February *I-29* was being refuelled from *U-488*, a 'Milch Cow', when she was spotted by an aircraft. She escaped any damage. While off Cape Finisterre *I-29* was caught on the surface at night by an aircraft carrying a Leigh Light. Again the submarine escaped undamaged. *I-29* finally arrived in the Bay of Biscay on 9th March.

Allied Intelligence was informed of the submarine's presence in the Bay. Two Tse-tse, HX904/E (S/Ldr Philips/F/O Thomson) and MM425/L (F/O Turner/F/O Curtis) with an escort of four FB VIs (HJ828/R, HP922/U, MM431/Z and LR349/Y) from 248 Squadron set out to attack the submarine on the 10th. With a cloud base of 1,500ft and visibility at 8-10 miles the vessel was finally spotted off Cape Penas just before 0920hrs with an escort of two German destroyers, *Z-23* and *ZH-1,* and two torpedo boats, *T-27* and *T-29*. Overhead there were eight Ju88C-6s from III./ZG 1 circling the ships down below. The Mosquitos initially approached from the north before circling

Tse-tse MM424/H was delivered in February 1944 and survived the war. Despite this it only flew 39 operational sorties. This aircraft retained the four machine guns.

around to the west and then further still to come in from out of the sun. The four FB VIs went for the Junkers in an attempt to draw them off the Tse-tse. F/Sgt Tongue, LR349/Y, claimed one of the Junkers shot down and F/O Forest claimed hits on another, as did F/Lt Jeffreys.

Of his attack on the Junkers F/Sgt Tongue wrote:

'As we dived through the clouds I was in line astern of F/O Forrest Z/248. Three Ju88s were in line astern ahead of us at about 1500ft and as we came in the last one broke off to port and turned to make cloud cover. F/O Forrest turned after it and I followed the other two, which had started a climbing turn to starboard, still holding formation. At between 400 and 500 yards range and angle off 30° I fired a two second burst at the second e/a and although no hits were observed it swung to port and turned back to starboard almost immediately. Again I fired a two second burst and saw hits on the port engine and the port side of the cockpit. Smoke began to stream from the engine and the e/a started to lose height and tried to turn into the convoy, either for covering fire or with the intention of ditching. Following him down we experienced erratic return fire from the position in the rear of the cockpit. A final burst brought a sheet of flame from the starboard engine of the e/a and another larger one from where the trailing edge of the port wing joined the fuselage. The e/a broke up and disappeared in the water leaving only a column of black smoke. No survivors or wreckage were seen on the surface.'

A view of Tse-tse MM424 taken in February 1944 possibly at Hatfield after flight acceptance trials and before delivery to 618 Squadron Special Detachment.

(Via Bruce Gordon)

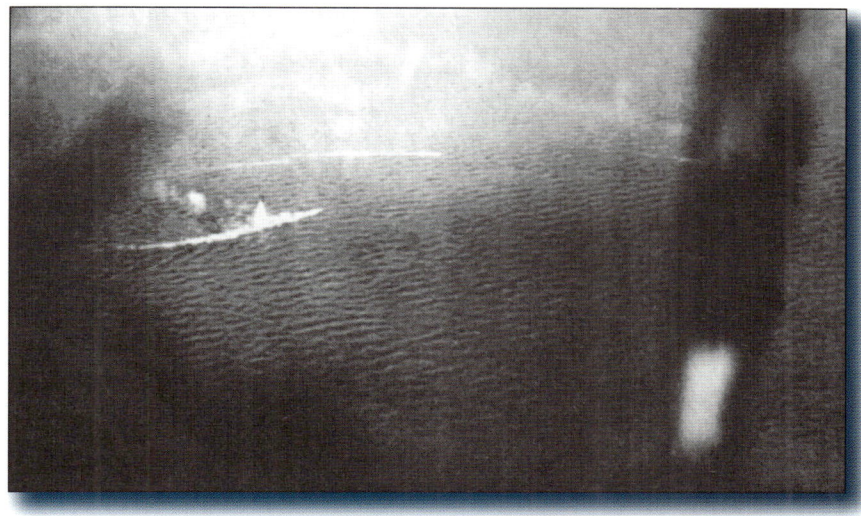

A dramatic shot showing U-976 under attack by 618 Squadron Special Detachment Tse-tses on 25th March 1944. Despite evasive manoeuvres U-976 was hit repeatedly and sank.

(Andy Bird)

Despite the flak coming up from the escorts the Tse-tse dived in to attack. S/Ldr Philips carried out four separate attacks and F/O Turner made two. A total of six hits were claimed on the submarine, although reports seem to indicate that the submarine suffered no actual damage. S/Ldr Phillips then fired on a destroyer and claimed 2-3 hits on the bridge, he then tangled with one of the Ju88s and claimed to have hit it after firing four shells from his Molins gun. The port engine was reportedly knocked out of the Junkers. According to German records 7/ZG 1 lost one Ju88 at 0924hrs. S/Ldr Phillips' aircraft, HX904/E, suffered category 'B' damage during this mission. A repair team from de Havilland arrived on the 14th to carry out the repair, but the Mosquito was not back in service until the 15th April.

U960 returns to harbour after another patrol. This U-boat was attacked and damaged by F/O Hilliard in Tse-tse HX903/I 27th March 1944.

(Andy Bird)

On 10th March 1944 a number of Ju88C-6s provided an aerial umbrella for the Japanese submarine I-29. This particular aircraft Wrk Nr 750965 2N+AA was shot down by a 157 Squadron Mosquito FBVI.

Later in the day at approximately 1700hrs a further wave of ten aircraft attacked the *I-29* and her escorts. Again the submarine would appeared to have escaped any damage. Ju88s from ZG 1 were in the air again providing an air umbrella for the Japanese submarine. This time they lost one of their number, Ju88C-6 Wrk Nr 750965 2N+AA of Stab./ZG 1, to a 157 Squadron Mosquito.

The *I-29* arrived safely at Lorient. For the journey home to Japan she was loaded with a HWK 509A-1 rocket motor, as used on the Me163 Komet, plus a Jumo 004B engine, as used on the Me262. She also carried plans for the Isotta-Fraschini torpedo boat engine, a V-1 'Buzz bomb' fuselage, TMC acoustic mines, bauxite and reportedly mercury-radium amalgam. During the journey home the American submarine *USS Sawfish* torpedoed and sank the *I-29* on 26th July 1944.

The 21st saw the Special Detachment attack a small motor vessel. MM425/L (F/O Turner/ F/O Curtis) came across a 1,500t tanker off the Spanish coast. The vessel was soon set on fire and it was later reported to have sunk. One of the escorting FB VIs flown by F/Sgt W R A Mowat and F/O R S Orr was hit by return fire from the ship and ditched just off the Cornish coast. F/O Orr's body was recovered the next day, although there was no sign of F/Sgt Mowat.

Encounters with Ju88s from ZG 1 were becoming more frequent. MM425/L (F/O Hilliard/W/O Hoyle) was approached by three of them on the 23rd, but these were driven off by the escorting 248 Squadron Mossies.

Success against the U-boats

The first successful sinking of a U-Boat occurred just off St Nazaire on the 25th. Two Tse-tse, HX903/I (F/O Hilliard/W/O Hoyle) and MM425/L (F/O Turner/F/O Curtis), were on patrol just below the cloud base when they spotted *U-976*, a Type VIIC, commanded by *Oblt* Raimund Tiesler, from 7 Flottille, on the surface eight miles away. One destroyer and two minesweepers accompanied the U-boat. The escorting Mosquitos increased power and carried out a number of strafing attacks on the escorts. The two Tse-tse swung round to attack from the port side. Ignoring the escorting destroyer and minesweepers Turner attacked first and knocked out one of the guns on the U-boat. He broke off and climbed for another attack. In all Turner made four attacks and used up all his ammo. Hilliard had the misfortune to suffer a gun jam after only firing one round. As well as knocking out the submarine's guns, hits were achieved on the forward deck and conning tower. Hit below the waterline the U-boat soon filled with water, which entered the battery compartment. Twenty-three minutes after the attack started the submarine sank beneath the waves leaving a large patch of oil on the surface. During the attack the Mosquitos came under AA fire from the nearby shore batteries. Four of the U-boat crew were killed in the attack but the escort vessels later picked up forty-nine survivors.

Two days later on the 27th another successful U-boat attack was carried out. Two Tse-tse, HX903/I (F/O Hilliard/W/O Hoyle) and MM425/L (F/O Turner/F/O Curtis), with an escort of six FB VIs, took off from Portreath at 0700hrs. At approximately 0900hrs the formation came across two surfaced U-Boats, *U-769* and *U-960*, with an escort of four minesweepers (including M4453, M4455 and M4457) and two *Sperrbrecher* ships, (*Sperrbrecher* 3 and *Sperrbrecher* 175) heading towards La Pallice. A *Sperrbrecher* was a converted merchant ship, which had concrete reinforced hulls to protect them from mines. These ships also bristled with AA guns. Usually they were mounted on high platforms to give them a better field of fire. The RAF regarded these ships as the most dangerous off all the German escorts and nick-named them "flak ships". Turning towards the coast the Mosquitos dived down on the convoy from up sun. The escorts put up a fierce anti-aircraft barrage, which the Mosquito crews bravely flew through. Hilliard

Z23 was part of the escort for the Japanese submarine I-29 on 11 March 1944. It was possibly hit by a number of 6pdr rounds.

received a 37mm cannon strike on the nose of his Tse-tse, but was able to continue with his attack and fire off about 7 rounds, claiming at least one hit on the conning tower of *U-960*. Turner dived on the same U-Boat and saw four of his shells hit the submarine. One shell had hit the conning tower and destroyed the attack periscope and injured 14 members of the crew, including the Commander, *Oberleutnant zur See* Heinrich. The badly damaged U-boat managed to make port. Three of the minesweepers also suffered various degrees of damage. M4455 was hit in the funnel, while the engine room and radio room were wrecked. Out of a crew of 33, one was killed and five others injured. One of the FB VIs, LR363/X, crash-landed back at base due to damaged received in the attack and four others suffered damage of varying degrees.

On 28th March the London Gazette announced the award of the Distinguished Service Order to S/Ldr A D Phillips DFC. Part of his citation read:

> 'This officer has completed a large number of sorties, many of which have demanded a high degree of skill and resolution. Recently, Squadron Leader Phillips flew the leading aircraft of a formation, which attacked an enemy naval force escorted by fighters. In the fight a U-boat and a surface vessel were hit, while 3 of the escorting aircraft were hit, one of them by Squadron Leader Phillips. This officer displayed fine qualities of leadership throughout and pressed home his attack with great determination. He played a good part in the success achieved. He has invariably displayed great courage and devotion to duty.'

The citation clearly mentions his part on the attack on the Japanese submarine *I-29* on the 10th March.

APRIL

On the 11th six Mosquitos from 248 and four from 151 Squadron escorted two Tse-tse, MM425/L (F/O Hamlett/ W/O Mudd) and HX903/I (F/O B C Roberts F/Sgt P Winsor) which had been ordered to carry out a patrol on Channel 'C'. One of the 248 Squadron Mosquitos was late in taking off. In an effort to catch up with the rest of the formation the pilot, F/Sgt P Hunt, attempted to cross a line of hills between Portreath and Predannack. Unfortunately he crashed into a hill which was covered in cloud. F/Sgt Hunt and his navigator, F/Sgt W W M Milne were killed instantly. F/O Hamlett also suffered problems and had to return to base, where he landed safely. The five remaining 248 Squadron Mosquitos were to provide anti-flak suppression for the Tse-tse. The four 151 Squadron machines would provide the top cover in case of any intervening *Luftwaffe* aircraft.

As the formation neared St Nazaire they came across a U-boat escorted by four minesweepers and a *Sperrbrecher*, plus 10 Ju88s from I/ZG1 patrolling overhead. The U-boat in question was *U-255*, a Type VIIC, commanded by *Oblt* Erich Harms, which had just returned from a six and a half week patrol. During this patrol Harms sank the USS *Leopold* from Convoy CU-16 on 9 March. F/Lt Roberts immediately pulled up to gain altitude and then dived down to attack the U-boat. Roberts saw his shell hit the water near the submarine but could not made any definite claims as to hitting the U-boat. The U-boat commander made a series of tight turns in order to throw the Tse-tse pilots off their aim. He also closed in on the escorting minesweepers to gain some protection from the attack. The other Mosquitos carried out attacks on the escorts, but almost immediately the Mosquito belonging to W/Cdr O Barron DFC was hit and burst into flames. It crashed into the sea taking both the pilot and navigator to their deaths. Another Mosquito was hit and crashed into the sea, killing both occupants. Noting the presence of the Ju88s one 248 Squadron Mosquito managed to get in a burst on one of the Junkers before their starboard engine burst into flames and the aircraft crashed into the sea. Both occupants managed to escape from the wreckage before it sank beneath the waves. After some two hours in the water they were both picked up by a French fishing boat. Another 248 Squadron crew, F/O T Scott and F/O G Yeates, shot down one of the Junkers. To confirm his success F/O Scott took a photo of the crashed aircraft. The *Sperrbrecher* was also hit and set on fire during the attack.

On the German side the Ju88 pilots had no hesitation in attacking the Mosquitos. Lt Gmelin dived into attack and straight away shot down a Mosquito. He then noticed his *Rottenflieger* (wingman) coming under attack by another Mosquito and it was shot down. As he closed in on the Mosquito one of his gunners, *Uffz* Zimmermann fired on the aircraft and shot it down in flames. He then came under attack from another Mosquito but managed to out fly it and get in behind to shoot it down into the sea. Attacked again from head on Gmelin fired a burst and this Mosquito also crashed into the sea. Evading further attacks Gmelin flew at low level back to base. The Ju88 flown by *Hptm* Moltrecht crashed while trying to pull out of a dive and a further Junkers was also lost.

For claims of five Mosquitos shot down I./ZG1 lost three Ju88s in this combat. Three Mosquitos were actually lost plus another that crashed on landing back at base. RAF claims were two destroyed, one probable and one damaged by 151 Squadron and one destroyed and one probable by 248 Squadron.

Later in the day 151 Squadron and I./ZG1 tangled again when they were searching for survivors from downed aircraft from the earlier combat. A further three Ju88s were claimed destroyed and two more damaged for the loss of one Mosquito and another damaged. The German pilots claimed four Mosquitos shot down.

U-255 survived the war and surrendered to the Allies on 10 May 1945. During a total of fifteen war patrols the U-boat sank 12 ships for a total of 55,920 tons.

W/Cdr A D Phillips was posted in to take over the command of 248 Squadron following the death of W/Cdr O J M Barron DFC. The next few days were relatively quiet for the Squadron.

The most feared of all the escort vessels were the Sperrbrechers. These were usually converted merchant ships that were armed to the teeth with AA guns. They were usually mounted on platforms to give the crews a better field of fire. The RAF pilots termed these vessels flak ships.

Two Mosquito FBVIs were lost on the 17th, one crashed on landing and the other with a hydraulic failure. As the pilot came into land with the wheels down but not locked both engines spluttered to a stop and the aircraft stalled into the ground. Plt Off Norrie suffered multiple abrasions and shock and F/Sgt White fractured his femur.

Further patrols were carried out during the month but no major engagements occurred. During the month a number of awards were made to the squadron. For his actions on 11th April F/O Yeates was awarded the Distinguished Flying Cross. The DFC was also awarded to Fly Offs D Curtiss, B C Roberts and D J Turner in recognition of gallantry and devotion to duty in the execution of air operations whilst serving with 248 Squadron Special Detachment.

The citation for F/O Desmond Curtis read:

'As navigator, this officer has participated in very many sorties and has proved himself to be a highly efficient member of aircraft crew. In March 1944, he took part in destructive attacks on a tanker. Four days later he was navigator of the leading aircraft of a formation, which attacked a convoy and probably sank a U-boat. Another two days afterwards, F/O Curtis was again the leading navigator of a bomber force, which attacked a large convoy. During the operation a U-boat was hit and damaged. In these operations this officer has displayed a high standard of navigational ability which contributed materially to the success obtained.'

MAY

The first three weeks of May proved to be one of continuous patrols, although no encounters of any kind were made with the enemy. All that were seen by the pilots were numerous fishing boats sailing to and from the Bay. On 18th May 1944 notification came through from 18 Group that 618 Squadron Special Detachment was to be disbanded and that the remaining Mosquitos and aircrew were to be transferred to 248 Squadron.

It was also decided to discontinue the production of the Mosquito FB XVIII Tse-tse. There were four in service with a number of others nearing completion. These would be completed but no more were ordered. This decision was based on the fact that the new rocket projectiles (RPs) were coming into use and could be fitted to any aircraft without major

U-255 under escort during the 11 April 1944 action. (Goss-Rauchbach archives).

modifications. 248 Squadron would continue to use the Tse-tse until they were all used up, when it would then revert to being totally equipped with Mosquito FB VIs. As the Germans knew that some Mosquitos carried a big gun there was no further reason for the strict security measures that were applied to 618 Squadron Special Detachment. For the time being the establishment of 248 Squadron was 20 FB VIs and 8 Tse-tses, formed into 'C' Flight.

618 Squadron Special Detachment crews posted to 248 Squadron:

Pilot	Navigator:
F/O A L Bonnet RCAF	F/O A M McNicol
F/O K Hamlett	W/O A Mudd
F/O D J Turner DFC	F/O D Curtis DFC
F/O A H Hilliard	W/O J Hoyle
F/O B C Roberts	W/O P Winsor

In the late evening of the 20th six FBVIs and two Tse-tse, HX903/I (F/O Hilliard/W/O Hoyle) and MM425/L (F/O J Green/F/O G B Forrest), were ordered out on an offensive patrol. They were to locate and attack a 'Jaguar' class destroyer believed to be in the area from 4830 N – 0520 W to 4835 N – 0338 W. The formation took off at 2110hrs and set course for the target area. At 2139hrs a number of Beaufighters were spotted and 10 minutes later an enemy formation was spotted. This comprised of seven minesweepers and the 'Jaguar' class destroyer. Heavy flak was experienced from these ships and as the failing light prevented any kind of attack from being carried out the formation set course for home.

The rest of the month carried on as before with numerous patrols with very little to show for it. Despite the lack of live targets routine training went on as normal and a total of 258 rounds of practice ammunition was fired. At this time there were four Tse-tse, HX903/I, HX904/E, MM242/H and MM425/L, on strength. This rather intensive training was required in order to keep the pilots in tune with their aircraft and weapon. Where possible each crew was assigned their own Tse-tse so they could get to know the individual quirks of the aircraft, that way there would be no surprises when it came to the real thing.

In early May HX904/E suffered some damage, possibly in a training sortie. The damage was considered light and the aircraft was deemed to be repairable on site. The Mosquito was returned to Squadron strength on the 21st, although it did not take part in any further operational sorties for that month.

JUNE

June would prove to be a busy month for 248 Squadron and the Tse-tse. Two more Tse-tse joined the Squadron during June, NT224/E1 on the 2nd and NT225/O on the 6th. In support of the D-Day landings they would fly on 22 operations, with a total of 42 sorties, which would be shared by five Tse-tse, HX903/I, HX904/E, MM424/H, MM425/L and NT225/O.

The first sortie of the month occurred on the 2nd when two Tse-tse, MM424/H (F/O Bonnet/F/O McNicol) and MM425/L (F/O Turner/F/O Curtis), were escorted by four FBVIs to carry out an anti-submarine patrol in the Isle de Yeux – Isle de Groix area. An hour and fifteen minutes after take off, at 2030hrs, a lone Ju88 was sighted flying on course 130° at 800ft. The Mosquitos gave chase but were unable to catch the fleeing Junkers. Twelve minutes later a three-ship convoy was sighted. One 800t minesweeper and a smaller escort vessel were fussing over a third vessel which was stationary in the water close to shore. Working their way up sun the two Tse-tse carried out an attack from the beam on the minesweeper. F/O Turner fired six rounds and achieved three hits below the waterline, two on the hull and one on the bridge. F/O Bonnet gained a further two strikes on the bridge. Two of the FBVIs, HJ828/R and HP908/P, carried out strafing runs on the minesweeper inflicting terrible damage with their 20mm and machine gun fire. As the Mosquitos broke off the attack and headed for home they were fired on by three armed trawlers, which failed to inflict any damage on the aircraft.

Next day the same two Tse-tse, this time with F/O Roberts and W/O Winsor in MM424/H, with four escorting FBVIs were sent to patrol the same area as the day before. They spotted a coaster of approximately 1,000t surrounded by yellow buoys. Heavy flak was experienced and the leader, F/O Roberts, decided the target was not significant enough to warrant an attack.

On the 4th June F/O W N Cosman, RCAF (pilot) and F/O L M Freedman (navigator) were posted to 248 Squadron from 132 OTU, East Fortune, Scotland. They were assigned to 'C' Flight and the Tse-tse. They were immediately put into an intensive training programme on flying and firing the 6pdr gun on the firing range.

On the 6th June the Allies landed in Normandy in what proved to be the largest single amphibious/air assault in the history of warfare. The Mosquitos of 248 Squadron played a big part in the operations from dawn 'til dusk. A total of twenty-five sorties were flown by 248 Squadron, three of them by the Tse-tse. The first sortie was at 0845hrs when MM424/H (F/O Roberts/W/O Winsor) was ordered to carry out an anti-U-boat/shipping patrol. Roberts was only 15 minutes into the flight when he received the order to return to base and that the patrol was cancelled. A later patrol at 1210hrs by two Tse-tse, MM424/H (F/O Roberts/F/O Curtis) and NT225/O (S/Ldr R A Atkinson/F/O R A Upton), carried out the same mission orders as the earlier cancelled sortie. In the Gironde Estuary

Ju88C-6 banks away to port. Note the heavy exhaust staining under the wings and tailplane.
(Goss-Rauchbach archives)

30

two small freighters were spotted but these were not attacked and the patrol returned to base, landing at 1634hrs.

The FBVIs from 248 flew four offensive patrols and at the end of the day put in claims for one Ju188 shot down and a destroyer badly damaged. All Mosquitos returned to base with no damage.

During the early morning of the 7th two Tse-tse, MM425/L (F/O Turner/F/O Curtis) and NT225/O (F/O Bonnet/F/O McNicol) took off at 0533hrs on an anti-U-boat patrol. Shortly before 0730hrs the aircraft were flying at 800ft when they spotted the tell-tale wake of a submarine. The U-boat was *U-212*, a type VIIC submarine commanded by *Kapt Lt* Helmuth Vogler, on the surface. Bonnet was unlucky enough to suffer a gun stoppage on his first pass on the U-boat. He carried out several dummy runs on the submarine to draw off the AA fire from Turner. Turner carried out his first pass firing 6 rounds of ammunition. He then climbed away to port and dived back to attack from the port beam firing another 6 rounds. He then carried out a third pass again from the port beam and again firing 6 rounds. By the time he came in for a fourth attack the submarine had crash-dived leaving one man in the water. Turner claimed to have hit the U-boat several times near the conning tower and below the waterline. Low cloud had prevented the pilots from making steeper attacks, which would have ensured penetration of the pressure hull. As it was a number of rounds may simply have bounced of the cylindrical hull. Turner suffered some damage to the port wing and engine nacelle during the attack but was able to fly back to base and land safely. The U-boat returned to La Pallice for repairs before continuing on her patrol. The following month *U-212* was sunk by Royal Navy frigates.

During an offensive patrol W/Cdr A D Phillips, HR138/Y, spotted a FW190 through broken cloud. He gave chase and fired off a number of short bursts, eventually hitting the fighter, which rolled over and dived into the sea killing the pilot.

An evening patrol on the 8th saw two Tse-tse, MM424/H (F/O Roberts/W/O Winsor) and NT225/O (S/Ldr Atkinson/F/O Upton), take off at 1940hrs. Over an hour later they were patrolling position 45°42'N 02°30'W when they spotted four small coastal freighters. On investigation they were found to be wearing Spanish markings. Later at 2222hrs they saw two small escorts off Ushant. Heavy flak was experienced from the two ships as well as shore batteries. With nothing else in the vicinity the aircraft set course for base and landed safely at 2320hrs.

On the 9th all four Tse-tse were off on an anti-shipping and reconnaissance patrol along with one FBVI. They were tasked to search for survivors from a sunken German destroyer and then proceed to Ile de Bas to locate and attack another destroyer which had run aground. The aircraft and crews were:

HX903/I		F/O Bonnet/F/O McNicol
NT225/O		S/Ldr Atkinson/F/O Upton
MM424/L		F/O Roberts/W/O Winsor
MM425/H		F/O Turner/F/O Curtis
HR138/Y	FBVI	W/Cdr Phillips/F/O Thomson

The aircraft set off at 1530hrs and set course for their patrol area. At 1624hrs a number of life rafts were spotted on the water containing numerous survivors from the German destroyer. To the northwest four destroyers were sighted and one of them was guided in to the life rafts. The aircraft continued on to their patrol area at Ile de Bas. Due to bad weather W/Cdr Phillips and F/O Bonnet became separated from the rest of the formation and had difficulty in reaching the area. After a number of attempts they succeeded and came across the grounded destroyer. They rejoined the rest of the formation and set course for base without attacking the destroyer.

As the formation approached base W/Cdr Phillips crossed under the formation and climbed to port. F/O Bonnet also turned to port and at 1,500ft over the edge of the airfield both aircraft collided. The starboard wing of Phillips' aircraft sliced through the tail of Bonnet's. HX903 dived out of control into the sea killing both pilot and navigator. Phillips was able to regain control of his aircraft and he carried out a successful landing.

A court of inquiry followed and it was found that no one was to blame and that it was an extremely unfortunate accident.

The next day at 1145hrs four FBVIs from 248 Squadron were on patrol off Ushant when they came across a U-Boat. This was *U-821* commanded by *Oblt* Ulrich Knackfuss from 1 *Flottille*. Numerous diving attacks were carried out by all four aircraft firing both 20mm and machine gun fire. An explosion was observed from the conning tower and a number of men were seen to jump overboard. They were able to inflict enough damage to keep it on the surface, thereby allowing a Liberator, 'K' from 206 Squadron, to come along and finish it off. There were a number of survivors from the U-Boat, who were rescued by a launch

During a follow up patrol by four 248 Squadron FBVIs the formation came across the launch, which was apparently rescuing survivors from the sunken U-boat. As the formation flew over the launch it opened fire with a machine gun, which hit HR117/J flown by F/Lt Jeffreys DFC and F/O Burden. The Mosquito was hit in the port wing, which caught fire. Jeffreys headed towards the coast but was unable to maintain control and the Mosquito crashed 50 yards from the coast. There were no survivors. The three remaining Mosquitos carried out strafing attacks on the launch inflicting some damage. Not far from the scene were two Tse-tse, MM425/L (F/O Roberts/W/O Winsor) and NT225/O (S/Ldr Atkinson/F/O Upton), which were on an anti-submarine patrol. These came over and attacked the launch as well. Both carried out several attacks and S/Ldr Atkinson claimed two hits out of eight rounds fired. F/O Roberts claimed five hits out of nine fired. They literally blew the launch to pieces, destroying it. There was one survivor from the launch and one from the U-boat.

Anti-submarine/shipping sweeps continued on an almost daily basis for the Tse-tse crews. Numerous enemy vessels were sighted but no attacks were carried out due to poor weather conditions or the targets being too heavily defended to warrant an attack. It wasn't until the 24th of the month that the 6 pdrs were fired in action.

A very early take-off at 0410hrs on the 24th by three FBVIs and two Tse-tse, MM424/H (F/O Cosman/Flt Off Freedman) and MM425/L (F/O Turner/F/O Curtis), saw the aircraft

A top view of Tse-tse NT225/O showing the camouflage pattern and D-Day stripes. This aircraft was shot down by enemy fighters on 7th December 1944 with the loss of F/O Cosman and F/O Freedman.

(Andy Bird)

arrive over Ile de Groix at 0500hrs. In the gloom of the early morning the aircraft had become separated. Turner was flying to the southwest of Pointe de Permarc'h when he came under fire from rather heavy flak. Up ahead Turner made out the silhouettes of some ships 3-4 mile away. He called up the rest of the aircraft and ordered them to attack. It was still too dark for Turner to use his 6pdr due to the fact that the muzzle flash would momentarily blind him, even though the rounds were filled with flashless cordite it still gave off a bright flash in dark conditions.

F/O Tonge, HR158/W, attacked the nearest ship, which was at the starboard rear of the formation, and opened fire with his cannon and machine guns to suppress the flak guns. As the light started to improve Turner carried out a number of shallow attacks and scored at least one hit on the ship, now identified as a minesweeper. A highly accurate and intense flak barrage was put up, not only from the ships but also from shore batteries. F/O Cosman also carried out a number of attacks on the same ship and although he fired off five rounds he couldn't determine if any hit the target. Two of the Mosquitos, HR158 and HP907, were hit and returned to base. Turner suffered from fuel feed problems with his drop tanks and returned to base early.

In the afternoon of the 29th two 248 Squadron FBVIs, LR347/T and MM430/Q, came across a 2,000t tanker with six escorts near Gironde. Both aircraft climbed to 8,000ft and dive-bombed the tanker. Unfortunately their aim was off and the bombs landed in the water 300 yards short of the tanker.

Later in the evening a combined effort from 235 and 248 Squadrons was sent out to attack the same convoy. This formation consisted of 10 FBVIs and 2 Tse-tse, MM424/H (F/O Cosman/F/O Freedman) and MM425/L (F/O Turner/F/O Curtis). From 235 came 6 FBVIs. Four of the FBVIs carried two 500lb bombs and the others were for anti-flak suppression. The convoy was duly found and the anti-flak aircraft went in. Fire was concentrated on the rear starboard escort vessels and one of them was badly damaged. The four bomb-carrying Mosquitos came next and all attacked individually, claiming a number of near misses. The last to attack were the Tse-tse. Turner came in first and lined up on the tanker. He opened fire at 2,500 yards and fired steadily until he broke off the attack at 50 yards. In all Turner fired 12 rounds of ammunition and a number of hits were seen. After about the ninth round smoke was seen coming from the bridge followed by an explosion. Cosman followed Turner but held his fire until 1,500 yards. After firing only one round his gun jammed, although he continued on with the attack and fired his machine guns at the tanker.

With the tanker belching black smoke the formation was ordered to reform and head back to base. When the pilots returned and were debriefed it was estimated that four or five of the escorts, identified as two minesweepers, two trawlers and two anti-submarine trawlers, as well as the tanker were damaged.

JULY

July started slowly for the Tse-tse pilots. Training continued as normal but few patrols were flown. Only seven sorties were carried out in the first ten days. Either nothing was sighted or bad weather precluded any attacks.

On the 11th a total of 16 Mosquitos escorted two Tse-tse, NT224/E1 (F/O Cosman/F/O Freedman) and NT225/O (F/O Turner/F/O Curtis), to the Goulet

As the war progressed the U-boats were to suffer more and more from air attacks. As a result the deck guns were removed and extra AA guns were mounted on the superstructure, which was extended back towards the stern. This Type VIIc-44 is a typical example.

F/O T Scott and F/O G Yeates, 248 Squadron, who shot down Ju88s on the 11th April and 31st July 1944. (Goss-Rauchbach archives).

de Brest, the narrow entrance to the port of Brest. Earlier in the day two U-boats, *U-415* and *U-963* left Brest. These two submarines were to form the group Pirat. At about 2230hrs the Mosquitos came across *U-963* surrounded by three M Class minesweepers and a *Sperrbrecher*, 1 mile from Toubinguet point. The vessels were still inside the boom defences and they together with the shore batteries put up an intense AA barrage. Undeterred F/O Cosman dived on the U-boat claiming two hits. As he broke off the attack Cosman fired a couple of shots at a minesweeper as well. Turner followed but was unable to line up on the U-boat so he fired off several rounds into the *Sperrbrecher* causing a small explosion. The other Mosquitos attacked the minesweepers, leaving two in flames and one badly damaged by cannon fire. All Mosquitos returned safely to base.

The U-boat suffered no actual damage during the attack and the next day both U-boats were recalled to Brest. Two days later on the 14th both U-boats again left Brest. Just as they passed the torpedo-net barrier *U-415* hit a mine and sank. Two members of the crew were killed but the rest were rescued. *U-963* survived the war but was scuttled by her crew on 20th May off the Portuguese coast. All 48 crewmembers were interned.

The next few days saw little in the way of action for the Tse-tse crews. The FBVIs on the other hand saw quite a bit of combat with the Luftwaffe. On the 21st they claimed one Do217 shot down with two others plus a He177 as probables. The next day another He177 was claimed as a probable. The last week in July saw two major convoy actions for the Tse-tse.

The crews were up early on the morning of the 27th. Crews were briefed for an anti-U-boat/shipping reconnaissance patrol and take of was scheduled for 0700hrs. Six FBVIs led by S/Ldr Randall would provide escort for the usual two Tse-tse, NT224/E1 (F/O Hilliard/ W/O Hoyle) and NT225/O (F/O Cosman/F/O Freedman). Not far from the enemy coast a convoy was spotted in position 47°10'N 02°32'W, which consisted of one 2,000t coaster, four-five TTAs and two-three auxiliaries. Bombs were dropped by the FBVIs, although those from HR261 hung up. The Tse-tse scored a number of hits on the coaster and one or two on the TTAs. Cannon and machine gun fire damaged other vessels. Light inaccurate flak was experienced but this was soon silenced on the vessels that were attacked. A number of fishing vessels were also present but these were not attacked. Some aircraft suffered slight damage but nothing too serious.

A similar patrol took place again the next day. Again six FBVIs escorted two Tse-tse, HX904/E (W/O G A MacAskill/ Sgt J W Keffers) and NT225/O (F/O Turner/ F/O Curtis). Just after 1000hrs a three-ship convoy, consisting of a TTA of 400t, a small coaster of 300t and a 500t coaster, was sighted. These ships were in line astern and stationary not far from the Ilse de Groix. The smaller of the coasters was attacked seven times and the other two ships each received two attacks. The Tse-tse achieved a number of hits on the small coaster and TTA. Flak was from the convoy was light but heavier flak was experienced from the Ilse de Groix. As they left the scene a column of black smoke reaching 2-300 feet in the air was seen coming from one of the coasters. On their return to base the pilots reckoned they had probably sunk the 500t coaster and badly damaged the TTA.

On the last day of the month a Ju188 was claimed shot down by FBVIs off Permarc'h Point.

AUGUST

August continued with almost daily anti-submarine/shipping patrols being carried out by the Tse-tse and FBVIs. On the 2nd August F/Sgt P M Griffiths/F/Sgt M S Smith failed to return from a sortie. It is possible that Griffiths became lost in heavy cloud and HP908/P, a FBVI, crashed into the sea.

W/Cdr Sise led twelve FBVIs and one Tse-tse, NT225/O (F/O Cosman/F/O Freedman) on an anti-shipping sweep from Ushant to Gironde on the 9th. One Mosquito, LR330, returned to base with undercarriage trouble. The rest carried on with the patrol and as they passed the Odet River four minesweepers and a floating dock were spotted. This formation was attacked and one of the minesweepers was left seriously damaged with the other three slightly damaged. F/Lt K Hamlett was wounded by flak during the attack and was escorted back to base by F/Lt L S Dobson.

Later that evening one of the Tse-tse, NT224/E1 (F/O Roberts/W/O Winsor), took off for a patrol towards Gironde. Escort was provided by 12 Mosquitos from 235 Squadron. Two coasters were seen to the South of Coubre Point and while the formation circled the coasters four Do217s were spotted in the near vicinity. The Mosquitos gave chase, and two of the Do217s were shot down with the other two claimed as damaged. The Dorniers were each equipped with glide bombs and were clearly heading for Allied shipping.

A successful sweep was carried out on the 12th. Again W/Cdr Sise led a formation of twelve FBVIs and two Tse-tse, NT224/E1 (F/O Roberts/W/O Winsor) and NT225/O (F/O Cosman/F/O Freedman), to the north of Gironde. At 0955hrs the formation attacked gun position as they crossed the coast to the south of the Mouth of Gironde, silencing them. Eleven minutes later a number of ships were sighted and the order to attack was given. In went the Tse-tse with 6pdrs hammering away. One minesweeper, M.370 from the 8th Minesweeper Flotilla, was hit and exploded, while three other vessels were damaged. One of these may have been M.4204, from the 42nd Auxiliary MS Flotilla, which was reported to have sunk after the attack. M.4204 was the ex-French fishing vessel

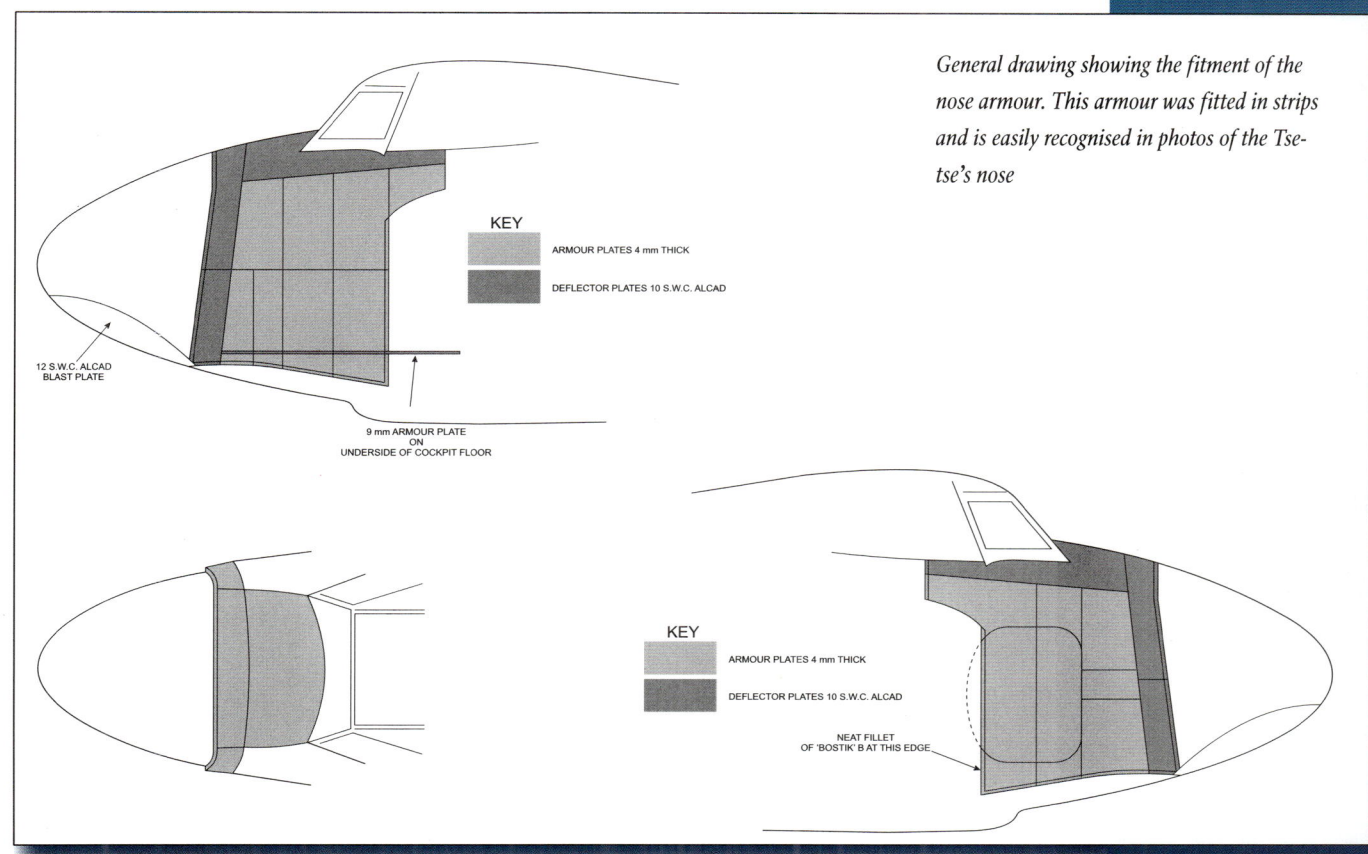

General drawing showing the fitment of the nose armour. This armour was fitted in strips and is easily recognised in photos of the Tse-tse's nose

KEY

ARMOUR PLATES 4 mm THICK

DEFLECTOR PLATES 10 S.W.C. ALCAD

12 S.W.C. ALCAD BLAST PLATE

9 mm ARMOUR PLATE ON UNDERSIDE OF COCKPIT FLOOR

KEY

ARMOUR PLATES 4 mm THICK

DEFLECTOR PLATES 10 S.W.C. ALCAD

NEAT FILLET OF 'BOSTIK' B AT THIS EDGE

Marie Thérèsa which had also served in the French Navy as *AD149*. A large 7,000t vessel *Sauerland* (*Sperrbrecher 7*) was also hit and subsequently sank, although this may have occurred at La Pallice. After the attack the aircraft split up and made their way home individually. Some aircraft had been hit by flak and LR347, from 248 Squadron, was seen to ditch near a group of escort vessels. The navigator, F/O W W Miller, was rescued while the pilot, F/Lt L S Dobson, was reported missing.

On the evening of the 14th two Tse-tse, HX904/E (F/O Turner/F/O Curtis) and NT225/0 (F/O Cosman/F/O Freedman) with 10 Mosquitos from 248 Squadron and 13 from 235 Squadron set off for the Gironde area looking for enemy shipping. While off Le Verdon S/Ldr Randall sighted a number of ships and gave the order to attack. The Tse-tse attacked and hit a destroyer that was in the middle of the channel. A number of explosions were observed and the flak from the destroyer soon stopped. A 4000t tanker was also hit by a mixture of cannon and machine gun fire and from near misses by depth charges and bombs. It was last seen on fire amidships and with smoke coming from the superstructure. One of the Tse-tse pilots also claimed hits on the tanker. A number of smaller vessels were also hit. The return fire from the ships was very accurate and four Mosquitos were shot down, one from 235 Squadron and three from 248.

Three days later an early morning sweep sighted a number of vessels at Le Verdon but no attacks were carried out. A second sweep off at 0840hrs came across a number of vessels at anchor in the Loire estuary. The leader of the formation, F/O G N E Yeates decided not to attack and headed for Ile de Yeu. Here a 600t vessel was sighted and Red Section was ordered to attack. The vessel was hit by cannon and machine gun fire. It also received a few rounds of 6pdr shells fired from NT225/O (F/O Cosman/F/O Freedman). The formation then broke off the attack and set course for base.

The 19th saw further action for the Tse-tse. Two of them, HX904/E (F/O Roberts/W/O Winsor) and NT225/O (F/O Cosman/F/O Freedman) were escorted by two FBVIs during a patrol from Permarsh Pt to La Pallice. Numerous vessels were sighted between the Gironde and La Pallice. Off Ile de Noir Montier a couple of minesweepers and two other vessels were sighted. Attacks were carried out on the minesweepers and numerous hits were claimed on both. Both Roberts and Cosman claimed at least 5-6 hits apiece on the vessels.

A Ju88H-1 of 3/123 under attack by a 248 Squadron Mosquito crewed by F/O Yeates/F/O Scott on 31 July. The Junkers was eventually shot down.

(Goss-Rauchbach archives)

Roberts and Cosman were out again two days later in the same aircraft. W/Cdr Sise led 8 FBVIs as well as 9 aircraft from 235 Squadron on an anti-shipping sweep down to Le Verdon. Two M Class minesweepers and one merchantman were sighted off Le Verdon heading upstream. All three vessels were attacked and plumes of water were seen all around the ships. One minesweeper was set on fire and an explosion was seen on the other one. All three ships were left smoking heavily and all were claimed seriously damaged. In fact minesweeper *M.292* sank soon after. Three Mosquitos from 248 Squadron were lost in this action. HR261/N crash-landed at St Mawgans, while LR340/K and HR922/U crashed at Vannesin France. Both crews survived.

On the 25th MM425/L (F/O Roberts/W/O Hoyle), took part in a strike against several minesweepers between Ile de Noirmontier and the mainland. Roberts was able to claim at least 8 6pdr hits on one of the minesweepers. It's possible he also hit another minesweeper

Eventually even the merchantmen were fitted with weapons. Here a 88mm or 105mm gun sits on the bow of this ship. (Author's Collection)

A typical freighter that plied its trade along the French coast, always in danger of being attacked. Author's Collection)

with 4 shells. Also during the day Tse-tse PZ252/Z1 was delivered to the squadron from Coastal Command Preparation Pool (CCPP). On the 31st two Tse-tse, PZ300/S1 and PZ301/T1, were also delivered from CCPP.

SEPTEMBER

During the first week in September yet another Tse-tse, PZ251/I was delivered to the squadron from CCPP.

On the 5th September three Mosquitos set out on an anti-shipping anti-U-boat patrol. The formation consisted of one Tse-tse, MM425/L (F/O Cosman/F/O Freedman), and two FBVIs. A number of small ships were sighted to the north of Port Louis off Lorient, but no attacks were carried out. Flak was experienced and one FBVI was damaged in the starboard engine nacelle and undercarriage.

Two days later the Tse-tse carried out their last sortie over the Bay of Biscay. Two Tse-tse, PZ251/I (F/Lt Turner/F/Lt Curtis) and NT225/O (F/O R S Driscoll/F/O S Hannant), with one FB VI carried out a patrol to the Gironde. Nothing was sighted until the formation reached Croisic Point and St Nazaire. Here several merchant vessels with a similar number of escorts were located. Visibility was poor and no further vessels were sighted, although a number of fires were seen in the direction of Brest.

The Squadron was released from duties for the next two days and on the 10th the Squadron moved to Banff.

BANFF STRIKE WING

With the Allied Armies now in Europe U-boats and shipping targets in the Bay of Biscay and English Channel were becoming scarce. A new Strike Wing was being formed at Banff, Scotland, and as a result 248 Squadron was posted there in mid-September. Here several Mosquito and Beaufighter squadrons would roam the fjords of Norway looking for suitable targets. Also at this time the Mosquitos were modified to carry eight rocket-projectiles (RPs). Initially 60lb semi-armour-piercing warheads were used but these proved in-effective in penetrating ship's outer hulls. Later 25lb solid armour-piercing warheads were used which would punch a hole 18 inches across into the hull of a ship.

A large strike force of 25 Mosquitos from 235 and 248 Squadrons, including four Tse-tse HX904/E (F/O D Peacock/F/O D C Field), MM424/H (F/O Driscoll/F/O Hannant), MM425/L (F/Lt Turner/F/Lt Curtis) and NT225/O (F/O Cosman/F/O Freedman), carried out a Rover patrol off the Norwegian coast on the 14th September. Seven Beaufighters from 144 Squadron and 12 from 404 Squadron, RCAF, provided an escort. Just off Kristiansund they spotted four merchant vessels, including *Iris* 3,323t and *Pompeji* 2,916t, with two escorts. During the attack the flak ship *VP.1608 Sülldorf*, 264t, was hit in the ammunition store. This eventually blew up and the ship sank with the loss of five men including the captain, *Oblt z S* Lembach. The *Pompeji* suffered a number of hits on one side and was later towed to Lillesan with a heavy list and on fire. The *Iris* was hit below the waterline and set on fire, while the other two merchant vessels were also damaged. The flak was very effective, forcing one Beaufighter 'O' of 404 Squadron to ditch with the loss of one crew member, the other was captured. Two other Beaufighters were damaged but managed to fly back to base, one with a dead engine and the other with a severely wounded pilot.

Three separate patrols were carried out on the 17th. Two of these patrols each involved two Tse-tse. No attacks were carried out due to bad weather conditions, although the formations were fired on by flak from shore installations.

During the 18th twelve Mosquitos, six from 248 and two from 235 Squadron, took off from Banff to carry out a patrol off the Norwegian coast. The formation was led by

W/Cdr Bill Sise. They were on the look out for a U-boat that was returning to base after experiencing some mechanical difficulties. The U-boat's distress signals had been picked up by a shore-based listening post. As the aircraft neared the Utvaer Lighthouse the lone U-Boat was spotted on the surface at a distance of some two miles. This was *U-867*, a Type IXC commanded by *Kapitan Zur see* Arved Muhlendahl. Due to the low cloud all the aircraft attacked from a height of 500ft. One of the first Mosquitos to attack was Tse-tse NT224/E1 (F/Lt Hilliard/W/O Hoyle). Diving in to attack Hilliard claimed several hits with his Molins gun. A second Tse-tse NT225/O (Plt Off Cosman/F/O Freedman) also carried out a number of attacks. Further hits were achieved by the other Mosquitos with 20mm and machine gun fire. Two of the aircraft were armed with depth charges and these were dropped within yards of the submarine. These attacks badly damaged the submarine, which was unable to submerge, and was last seen listing to port. During this attack an AA battery from a nearby island opened fire on the attacking aircraft.

Further searches were carried out to look for the damaged submarine but these all failed to locate the stricken vessel. The next day it was found by a patrolling Liberator from 224 Squadron and sunk with all hands. On the 22nd Tse-tse PZ251/I (F/O Cosman/ F/O Freedman) had to return from a patrol early after suffering problems with its starboard engine. The Tse-tse was escorted back by two FBVIs and made a safe landing at Drem airfield.

Two Tse-tse from 'C' Flight, PZ251/I (F/Lt Turner/ F/Lt Curtis) and HX904/E (F/O Cosman/Freedman), were part of a formation of six aircraft that took part in a Rover patrol between Utvaer Light and Marsten Light on the 24th. The aircraft took off at 1200hrs and two hours later they crossed the coast at Utvaer. Here a stationary coaster fired on them. Continuing along the coast a two-ship convoy was soon sighted in Hjelte Fjord off Toft. The convoy consisted of the *Storesund* and the *VP.5502 Biber* from the 55th *Vorposten Flotille*. The *Biber* was the ex-Norwegian whaler *Veslefrik* that had been taken over by the Germans and converted into an escort vessel armed with 1 x 88mm, 3 x 20mm, 1x machine gun and 2 x *Rakten Geschüss* (RAG-anti-aircraft rockets).

S/Ldr Maurice took the formation up to 6,000 feet before commencing the attack. The first ship to be hit was the *Biber*, which came under attack from a Tse-tse. A number of hits were achieved with the Molins gun and the ship sank almost immediately.

A close up of the nose of a 248 Squadron Tse-tse. Note the additional strips of armour plating around the nose and crew entry door. This particular aircraft does not have the exhaust shrouds that were fitted to most of the Tse-tse and it retained all four machine guns.

(Andy Bird)

One crewman was killed and seven others injured, four of them seriously, one of them being the Captain of the vessel *Obersteuermann der Reserve* Kowski. The *Storesund* was then selected for attack and was left in flames. One of the crew, Annstein Gismarvik, was killed during the attack. It has been claimed that the vessel was sunk during this operation. This is not the case, as she was repaired and used post war until scrapped in Belgium in 1954. One of the attackers, 'R' from 248 Squadron, was hit by flak, which knocked out a chunk of the leading edge from one of the wings. Despite this damage the aircraft was able to fly back and land safely at Banff.

At 1253hrs another formation of Mosquitos took off from Banff. Two Tse-tse crews (F/O Hilliard/W/O Hoyle and F/O K C Wing RCAF/F/Sgt Shield RAAF) were part of the formation as well. The identity of the Tse-tse they were flying has not yet been identified. Their patrol line was the same as the earlier flight, Utvaer-Marstein. Off Marstein a small coaster fired on them with light flak and RAG. At 1507hrs two vessels were sighted and identified as a 500t TTA and a 400t minesweeper. They were in fact two patrol vessels *NB-07 Bison* and *NB.14 Hornisse*. All aircraft attacked with 20mm and 6pdr. *Bison* took a number of hits to the bridge and was set on fire. It was later beached. Heavy and light flak was experienced and all the attackers suffered damage of one degree or another. Both Tse-tse were hit in the wings and fuselage. All aircraft reached base safely.

The squadron was released from duties for the next couple of days. On the 27th two patrols were carried out and apart from receiving some accurate flak from shore batteries no shipping was attacked. A number of single-engined aircraft were spotted but none of these came anywhere near the Mosquitos.

The next day F/Lt L Bacon led half a dozen aircraft, including HX904/E (F/O Cosman/F/O Freedman) and MM425/L (F/O Woodcock/F/O Vacher), on a Rover patrol from Lista to Kristiansand South. Near Lista two ships were spotted and the formation readied itself for the attack. The minesweeper *NK.02 Dragoner* and torpedo boat *Kjell* were both hit by Tse-tse shells as well as the usual 20mm and machine gun fire plus a number of 500lb bombs. One of the 248 Squadron aircraft, 'K', even dropped depth charges on the vessels. After suffering numerous hits the *Dragoner* slowly settled lower and lower in the water until she eventually sank with the loss of 18 of the crew. All Mosquitos returned to base without any major damage.

The Tse-tse were out again on the 30th, when three of them, HX904/E (F/O Woodcock/ F/O Vacher), MM424/H (F/O Roberts/W/O Windsor) and NT225/O (F/O Wing/F/Sgt Shield), along with three FB VIs carried out an anti-U-boat sweep. A number of wrecks were sighted off Lister and the formation came under accurate heavy flak from the southern end of the Peninsula and from Mandel.

OCTOBER

A number of sorties took place on the 8th October involving small numbers of Mosquitos. One such flight involved a Tse-tse MM424/H (F/O Woodcock/F/O Vacher) and a FB VI (F/Lt Nicholls/F/O Hanson), which were to carry out an anti-U-boat patrol. At 1345 hrs just north of Markein light three vessels were spotted which were identified as two M Class minesweepers and one TTA. About one minute later a 3,000t merchant vessel and three more M Class minesweepers were spotted. All four vessels opened fire on the two Mosquitos. The fire extinguishers in Nicholl's Mosquito went off, and thinking his engines had been hit he turned away. After a few minutes he turned back as his engines appeared to be undamaged. A little later a tanker and three TTAs were spotted. As the aircraft closed in a single-engined fighter approached the Mosquitos. The aircraft, believed to be a Fw190 (possibly from JG5) closed in on the Tse-tse, fired a two-second burst, and then turned away.

Nicholls decided to attack one of the TTAs that was escorting the tanker. Both aircraft attacked and Woodcock was able to get in some good hits with his 6 pdr. Nicholls also sprayed the vessel with 20mm and machine gun fire, which was last seen billowing black smoke, which rose above the surrounding mountains. Flak was encountered from all the escorts but none hit the Mosquitos.

During the morning of the 17th lone Mosquitos from 333 Squadron had taken off to carry out reconnaissance missions along the Norwegian coast. A number of vessels were sighted near Gossen. As a result of these sightings a formation of 9 Mosquitos from 235 and 9 from 248 Squadron took off to carry out an armed patrol near Gossen. Among the 248 Squadron aircraft were four Tse-tse:

Two 6pdr shells streak towards their target during a strike off the Norwegian coast. Two Mosquitos can be seen pulling away after attacking ships in the harbour.

(Andy Bird)

HX904/E   F/Lt S B L Beattie/F/Lt D J Cutts
MM424/H   F/O Roberts/W/O Winsor
NT225/0   F/O Woodcock/F/O Vacher
PZ346/Z   Flt Off wing/F/Sgt Shield

As they approached Gossen a lone vessel, *VP.6801 Viking*, was spotted through the murky conditions. Three aircraft from 248 Squadron, including Tse-tse PZ346/Z, were ordered to attack the vessel. The *Viking* was smothered in machine gun and cannon fire. F/O King claimed two hits with his 6pdr, one of which hit just below the funnel. On fire and taking in water the *Viking* was subsequently beached at Hogstenen. All aircraft returned to base.

At 1420hrs on the 19th U-boat *U-382*, commanded by *Oblt* Hans-Dietrich Wilke met up with an escort vessel, *VP5116 Unitas I*, to be escorted into Bergen.

An hour earlier 9 Mosquitos from 235 Squadron, one from 333 Squadron and 11 from 248 Squadron took off at 1315hrs for an armed patrol in the vicinity

An armed trawler hugs the coast as it escorts a convoy down the Norwegian coast.

(Paul Sedal)

The Banff Strike Wing operated the Tse-tse alongside the standard Mosquito FB VI. Here we see HR414/NE-L of 143 Squadron sitting at dispersal.

(Paul Taylor)

of Hjeltefjord. Within the 248 Squadron formation were four Tse-tse:

HX904/E   F/Lt Beattie/F/Lt Cutts
MM424/H   F/O Roberts/W/O Winsor
PZ300/S1   F/O Driscoll/F/O Hannant
PZ301/T1   F/O Peacock/F/O Field

At 1528hrs they came across convoy Be-944-Al consisting of three vessels. The convoy was made up of the tug *Süderpiep* 323t, which was towing a barge *BSL 1* 3,500t, carrying a cargo of 68,600 bags of cement, and one escort vessel, *VP.5111 Odin*. The pilots mistakenly reported the barge as a 4,000t tanker. Two miles ahead of this convoy was *U-382* and her escort. On sighting the Mosquitos the U-boat dived, unseen by the Mosquito pilots, who then assumed that *VP.5116* was part of the convoy escort. *VP.5116* was the first vessel to be attacked. It was raked with 6 pdr, 20mm and machine gun fire. F/Lt Beattie claimed four hits with his 6pdr. A number of fires broke out and several of the crew were injured in the attack. The *Süderpiep*, and the barge *BSL 1*, were both damaged. Casualties suffered during the attack included Arne Frantzen, captain of the barge, Capt Andreas Johannessen and Martin Frøkedal, both from *Süderpiep*. The barge eventually sank.

It has often been reported that during this action a U-boat surfaced in the middle of the battle and shot down one of the Mosquitos. According to the U-boat's War Diary *U-382* did surface, but this was after the attack and they did not shoot at any aircraft. *Oblt* Wilke took on board

This escort is a more substantial minesweeper. These ships were heavily armed with machine guns, 20mm, 37mm and 88mm anti-aircraft guns and could put up a lethal barrage.
(Paul Sedal)

Some convoys had more escorts than merchant vessels, such was the fear of the roving Mosquitos.

(Paul Sedal)

A German escort vessel shepherds a convoy off the Norwegian coast. These escorts were usually minesweepers, patrol boats and converted trawlers and whalers. **(Paul Sedal)**

several injured crew members from *VP5116* and headed off to Bergen, where they were taken to hospital.

One Mosquito from 235 Squadron was lost, although whether it was to flak from the ships or from the shore is unclear. The pilot, W/O Ian Martin DFC was killed but the navigator, W/O Ian Ramsay managed to escape from the sinking aircraft. He scrambled into the life raft and was later picked up and taken into captivity.

U-382 was involved in a collision with another U-boat a few days later and in January 1945 she was sunk by the RAF at the entrance to Wilhelmshaven, Germany.

The 21st saw 4 Mosquitos from 235 Squadron, 1 from 333 Squadron and 7 from 248 Squadron, including Tse-tse NT224/E1 (F/O Peacock/F/O Field), NT225/O (F/O Woodcock/F/O Vacher), PZ251/I (F/O Driscoll/F/O Hannant) and PZ252/Z1 (F/O J M Hayton/F/O C H Day) along with 6 Beaufighters from 404 Squadron, set out on a Rover patrol to Stadtlandet. Here no targets were seen so one section led by F/Lt Power from 404 Squadron headed south. Further south a lone Mosquito from 333 Squadron reported shipping at Haugesend Harbour. Here the two sections joined forces and prepared to attack the vessels. At anchor in the harbour were the *Eckenheim* of 1923t, and *Vestra* of 1432t. The *Vestra* was on her way from Nordmøre to Sauda with a cargo of limestone. Although crewed by Norwegians the vessel's flak guns were manned by German soldiers. Beaufighters from 404 Squadron went in first firing rockets into the *Eckenheim*. A large number of hits were seen on the superstructure plus a few below the waterline. The bridge and upper works were riddled with 20mm cannon fire. Next came the Mosquitos, including the Tse-tse. At least four 6pdr hits were claimed. Badly holed and on fire, the *Eckenheim* started to take on water. During a second attack by a Tse-tse a further two hits were claimed. The *Eckenheim* was so badly damaged that it took the Germans two months to make her seaworthy.

Next came the turn of the *Vestra*, hit by rockets and cannon fire the vessel quickly sank. The attack happened so quickly that the gun crews never had time to get to their posts. All the crew, including the gunners, escaped from the sinking ship with no casualties.

A third vessel, the *Taube*, was also hit and left in a damaged condition. Two of the escorts *VP.5310* and *S.11* were also attacked and damaged. Heavy flak from the ships and from shore batteries was encountered and as a result one of the Tse-tse, PZ251/I, was shot down. F/O Driscoll and F/O Hannant were both killed. A Beaufighter also received some damage, although it returned to base safely, as did all other attacking aircraft.

Just before midday on the 23rd W/Cdr Atkinson led a 21-strong formation of aircraft from 235 and 248 Squadrons, including Tse-tse MM242/H (F/O Roberts/W/O Winsor), NT224/E1 (F/O Hilliard/Wt Of Hoyle), NT225/O (F/Lt Beattie/F/Lt Cutts) and PZ300/S1 (F/O Woodcock/F/O Vacher), to patrol the waters between Marstein Light and Ålesund. As they approached Hjeltefjord five merchant vessels were encountered along with a number of flak ships and other smaller vessels.

As the order came over the R/T 'Attack, attack, attack' the aircraft dived on the vessels below. One of the escorts, a tug *VP.5506 Zick*, came in for some close attention. Zick was the former Norwegian Navy ship *Tryyg*, which had been scuttled in April 1940. It was subsequently raised, fitted with a number of AA guns and put into service as an escort vessel. The *Zick* was badly damaged in the attack and eventually sank. The vessels *Biri*, *Sheen*, *Aasenfjord*, *Vulcanus*, and *Speer 14* all suffered various degrees of damage during the attack. F/Lt Beattie claimed one hit. Most of the vessels hit were left emitting great clouds of grey and black smoke. Some sources state that *Biri* sank the next day due to the damage inflicted in the attack.

Not only did the attacking aircraft have to suffer AA from the vessels but also from shore batteries at Hjeltfjord as well. Tse-tse PZ300/S1 was hit in the port wing by an AA shell, but the damage was not serious.

In October Air Chief Marshall Sholto Douglas requested more Tse-tse Mosquitos. However, following the successful trials of the rocket projectile he reversed his decision and recommended that further conversions be abandoned, this was agreed by the Chief of Air Staff. It was also decided that the remaining Tse-tse would be phased out of service rather than being retired by a specific date.

Intensive training took place at Banff on the new rocket projectiles and the first mission was flown on 26th October. On the 28th Tse-tse PZ346/Z was delivered to the squadron from CCPP.

A number of Mosquitos from 248 Squadron were off Lista on the 29th when they spotted a U-boat on the surface. F/O Woodcock, flying a Tse-tse, carried out two passes on the submarine, firing off eight 6pdr shells. He claimed to have scored two hits. The other Mosquitos also attacked with cannon and depth charges. The only U-boat thought to have been in the area at that time was *U-1061*. The commander reported being attacked on two separate occasions by aircraft the day after the Mosquito attack. Either someone mixed up the dates or the true victim of the Mosquitos has yet to be discovered.

On the 30th two Tse-tse, NT225/O (F/O Cosman/F/O Freedman) and PZ301 (F/O Hayton/F/O Day), were in formation with two Mosquitos from 235 Squadron. They were to carry out an anti-U-boat sweep from Makstein Light to Utvaer. Near Makstein Light a small tug with a trawler towing a barge were spotted but not attacked. Not long after a Ju88 was sighted at 8,000ft to the northwest of Holmengrå at a range of 3-4 miles. Cosman turned onto a converging course and carried out an attack. He opened fire with his Molins gun and fired off 6 rounds as well as a number of machine gun rounds. No hits were observed. Next it was the turn of one of the 235 Squadron Mosquitos. The Junkers was severely damaged by

A typical escort vessel as used on the Norwegian convoy routes. They simply bristled with AA guns. Most were converted trawlers, whalers and tugs. Although the guns were manned by Germans the crews were normally Norwegians.

the 20mm and machine gun fire. Cosman came in for another attack and fired off a further two rounds from his 6pdr at a range of 500yds, again no hits were observed. Finally Hayton came into attack from dead astern. The Junkers blew up and crashed into the sea. There were no survivors.

The Ju88 (D7+UH) may have been from *Westa 3*, which lost one aircraft to enemy action on the 30th. There were four crewmembers on board, *Ass* Werner Hast, *Ogfr* Walter Hasse, *Fw* Josef Riedmeier and *Uffz* Karl E Mazur. Two of the bodies, those of Hast and Hasse, were recovered by Norwegian fishermen and were buried at Bergen-Solheim.

NOVEMBER

On the 12th November a force of Royal Navy ships attacked a German convoy off Norway and sank 8 out of the 11 ships. The next day the Banff and Dallachy Strike Wings were ordered to attack the remaining three ships. A force of 8 Beaufighters and 18 Mosquitos took off in wet conditions to seek out the ships. As the force approached Rekefjord they spotted the convoy through a clear patch of weather. The convoy now consisted of 6 ships, the *Palermo*, *Rosenberg I* and four escorts.

The Strike Force climbed to around 1,500ft and selected their targets. The first to be hit was the escort vessel *R32*. 20mm cannon fire and rockets tore into the wooden superstructure causing extensive damage. The ship eventually foundered and sank. Next it was the *Rosenberg I* to suffer under the impact of rockets and cannon fire, although badly damaged the vessel remained afloat. Not so lucky was the air sea rescue vessel, *Fl.B 529* of 75t, which sank under the impact of several hits. The escort vessel *UJ1754* was also damaged. AA fire hit a number of aircraft but most of the damage was light and all aircraft returned to their respective bases.

During the day a Tse-tse landed with a round jammed in the breach. As the ground crew were trying to figure out what to do it went off. A number of airmen were caught in the muzzle blast and suffered slight burns. It is not clear whether the Tse-tse was on a training sortie or part of the strike force which attacked the convoy near Rekefjord.

Two Tse-tse PZ252/Z1 (F/O Peacock/F/O Field) and PZ346/Z (F/O Roberts/W/O Winsor) were part of a large formation of Mosquitos that went out on an anti-shipping reconnaissance on the 14th. W/Cdr Atkinson led the formation and it wasn't long before

A photo from a strike by 248 Squadron on an M-Class minesweeper and two trawlers in the Gironde Estuary. The exact date is not know but during these missions at least 1-2 Tse-tse accompanied each strike. As can be seen it was a very dangerous place to be. Pilots not only had to avoid the flak but also fire from other aircraft as pilot's jockeyed for position.

(IWM negative C4551)

they spotted a convoy of three ships near Dingja. These were the *Gula*, a small 263t cargo/passenger ship and the 177t *Sardinen*, which was towing the barge *Camperfehn*. Coming into attack the pilots concentrated on the *Gula* and *Sardinen*. On board the *Gula* were 30 passengers from Bergen. These included about 15 children who were being evacuated to a safer area. During the attack two female passengers were killed and two more injured. Three of the crew, Boatswain Tyvold, 2nd Mate Thorsen and Able Seaman Strandenæs were also injured. A fire broke out and the ship was beached at Dingja. The *Sardinen* was also badly hit, as was the *Camperfehn*. Stoker Frederik Oluf Wallin was killed and both vessels sank in shallow water. Light flak was experienced but none hit the attackers and all aircraft returned to base safely.

On the 17th the London Gazette announced the award of the DFC to F/O William Nathan Cosman. Part of the citation read:

'This officer, now on his second operational tour, has unfailingly pressed home his attacks with outstanding courage and determination. He has taken part in attacks on submarines, a destroyer and minesweepers. F/O Cosman has displayed great skill and his devotion to duty has been of a high order'

On the 21st a large strike was planned for Aalesund Harbour. From Banff came Mosquitos from 235 Squadron (12), 143 Squadron (6), 248 Squadron (14) and 333 Squadron (1). From Dallachy came the Beaufighters of 455 Squadron (11), 404 Squadron (12), 489 Squadron (6) and 144 Squadron (13). The whole formation was escorted by 12 Mustangs from 315 Squadron. A total of 6 Tse-tse were made ready for the sortie, whose crews were:

MM424/H	F/O Roberts/W/O Winsor
MM425/L	F/O King/F/Sgt Shield
NT225/O	F/O Cosman/F/O Freedman
PZ252/Z1	F/O Hayton/F/O Day
PZ301/T1	F/O Peacock/F/O Field
PZ346/Z	F/Lt Turner/F/Lt Curtis

The Mosquito from 333 Squadron flew ahead of the formation to investigate the approaches to the harbour and the harbour itself. Unfortunately only small vessels were spotted and with the visibility deteriorating the strike was aborted and all aircraft turned for home. F/O Peacock landed at Wick.

In 1989 a memorial was unveiled in a lay-by on the Inverness to Fraserburgh road. The memorial is dedicated to the six Squadrons (143, 144, 235, 248, 333 and 404) which flew with the Banff Strike Wing. The inscription on the memorial reads:

This memorial commemorates the men and women who served with the six multi-national squadrons which formed the Banff Strike Wing at RAF Banff between September 1944 and May 1945. Under the command of group captain the Hon. Max Aitken the mixed Mosquito and Beaufighter units mounted concentrated attacks on German surface vessels and U-boats in the North Sea and along the Norwegian coast. Their success in the closing months of World War II was important in the defeat of Germany and strike wing aircraft operating from the airfield near here inflicted heavy damage on enemy shipping and supply routes. Many thousands of tons of vital iron ore and other supplies were lost to the German forces as a result of rocket and cannon attacks carried out by this gallant strike wing. Losses amongst RAF commonwealth and Norwegian squadrons were high. More than 80 aircrew gave their lives flying with the RAF Banff Strike Wing.

The smaller stone behind the memorial is dedicated to 14 (Pilot) Advanced Flying Unit, which operated from Banff from August 1943 until August 1944 when the station was turned over to the Strike Wing.

In the late afternoon of the 29th two FBVIs and two Tse-tse, MM424/H (F/O Woodcock/F/O Vacher) and PZ301/T1 (F/O King/F/Sgt Shield), along with two FBVIs from 143 Squadron set out on an anti-U-boat patrol in the vicinity of Lister. In the gathering gloom the conning tower of a U-boat was spotted. First to attack were the FB VIs which opened fire with cannons and machine guns. F/O Woodcock opened fire with his 6 pdr and loosed off eight rounds claiming two hits. F/O King also attacked and claimed one hit. At this point the U-boat dived and was lost from view.

The U-boat was probably *U-170*, a Type IXC/40 from the 33 U-boat Flotilla based at Flensburg. The U-boat's commander, Oblt Hans-Gerold Hauber, reported seeing 8 enemy aircraft in square AN35 at 1628hrs on the 29th and crash-dived.

DECEMBER

On the 5th December a strike was laid on after a number of vessels were spotted holed up in Voldafjord. A formation of 34 Mosquitos was led by W/Cdr Bill Sise. The contribution from 248 Squadron consisted of ten FBVIs and four Tse-tse, MM424/H (F/O Woodcock/F/O Vacher), NT224/E1 (F/O Cosman/F/O Freedman), PZ252/Z1 (F/O Hayton/F/O Day) and PZ301/T1 (F/O Wing/F/Sgt Shield). Crossing the North Sea at wave top height the formation made landfall at Nordgulen Fjord. Lying at anchor were four merchant ships, three TTAs and a large tug plus other smaller vessels. Although not the intended target, Sise ordered F/O Woodcock and F/O Cosman to go down and attack them.

The two pilots broke formation and, braving the fierce AA fire that was directed at them, attacked the vessels below. Woodcock attacked a 4,000t vessel and fired off 15 rounds at it claiming three hits on the superstructure. Cosman attacked a smaller 3,000t vessel and fired off 6 rounds claiming two hits to its superstructure. They then rejoined the formation and continued on patrol.

Arriving over their intended target a number of vessels were spotted in the Fjord. They were anchored so close to the mountain sides that to attack them would have been fool-hardy and dangerous. Sise decided to head back to Nordgulen Fjord and carry out a further attack on the vessels they had seen earlier. The vessels were actually from two separate convoys that had anchored at the fjord for the night - a northbound convoy of three ships plus four escorts and a southbound convoy of one ship being towed by two tugs with three escorts.

The vessels in the fjord were:

Name	Type	Tonnage	Convoy	Armament
Tucaman	Freighter	4,621t	north	1x 20mm
Magdalena	Freighter	3,273t	north	
Helene Russ	Freighter	995t	north	
VP.5102	Flak ship		north	
VP.5111	Flak ship		north	
VP.5305	Flak ship		north	
VP.5306	Flak ship		north	
Ostland	Freighter	5,273t	south	1x 88mm, 2x 37mm, 2x 20mm, 4x RAG.
Aasenfjord	Armed Tug	571t	south	1x 20mm, 2x mg34
Fairplay X	Armed Tug		south	
VP.5109	Flak ship		south	
VP.5308	Flak ship		south	
VP.5310	Flak ship		south	
Vesla	Freighter	1,108t		1x 20mm, 2x mg34

The Vesla was not involved with any of the two convoys she was just unlucky enough to be in the fjord at the time of the attack.

The crews on board these vessels were still recovering from the earlier attack when the unmistakable sound of engines could be heard. The gun crews rushed to their posts and prepared to meet the onslaught. As the Mosquitos attacked they were met by a barrage of 20mm and 37mm fire from the various ships at anchor as well as heavier fire from 88mm guns of the shore batteries. With 30 plus aircraft all jostling for a firing position there was also a grave danger from collision. Cosman dived in on a 2,500t vessel and caused severe damage to it, claiming 6 hits and leaving the vessel on fire. F/O Wing was next and attacked a 3,000t ship and claimed a total of 9 hits. In a matter on minutes it was all over. The Mosquitos headed for home leaving several vessels damaged and on fire. The *Aasenfjord* suffered damage to the bridge and superstructure and *Magdalena* was set on fire. *Tucaman* had one of her 20mm AA guns put out of action, while the *Ostland*, *Vesla* and *Helene Russ* were also damaged. *Helene Russ* carried a cargo of AA ammunition, which started to explode, the crew braved these explosions to try and save their ship, which they eventually did.

The cost to the attackers was one Mosquito from 248 Squadron shot down with the loss of F/Lt L M Collins and F/O R H Hurn. Several more aircraft were damaged. On the return flight F/O Hayton (PZ252/Z1) landed at Sumburgh. A guide as to how much flak was thrown up against the Mosquitos can be taken from the War Diary of the escort vessel VP5109. Armed with 1x88mm, 1x37mm and 3x20mm, the vessel fired a total of 31x88mm rounds, 113x37mm rounds and 388x20mm rounds. All this from one ship in an action that lasted maybe 3-5 minutes.

In an effort to provide some form of protection against these raids the Luftwaffe moved JG5 to Southern Norway. The unit was equipped with Bf109s and Fw190s.

Two days later on the 7th a large strike by 25 Mosquitos from Banff and 40 Beaufighters from Dallachy was ordered to undertake an anti-shipping sweep in the Aalesund area. Twelve Mustangs from 315 Polish Squadron provided escort. 248 Squadron's contribution to this formation was six FBVIs and four Tse-tse. A total of seventy-eight aircraft formed up over Banff before setting course for Norway. Also accompanying the strike force were two Air Sea Rescue Warwicks from 279 Squadron. Not long into the journey a number of Mosquitos and Beaufighters had to return to base with varying degrees of mechanical trouble. Two of the returning Mosquitos were from 248 Squadron, plus another one that acted as escort.

Flying ahead of the formation was a Mosquito from 143 Squadron. The pilot, F/Lt Quelch, had been ordered to carry out a reconnaissance of Aalesund. Here he spotted

Mustang III FB353 PK-H during a North Sea escort mission to Norway. An ex-316 Squadron machine, it still wears the distinctive scoreboard of kill and mission markings known from other 316 aircraft.Polish Mustangs escorted Banff Wing Mosquitoes in early December 1944.

(Andy Thomas coll via Michał Mucha)

two vessels at anchor plus another two to the north of the main anchorage. This information was radioed back to the strike force. As this force neared the coast they climbed to 4,000ft. At this height they discovered they were too far to the north of their intended landfall. They eventually made landfall about 5 mile east of Gossen. On Gossen was a Luftwaffe fighter base, which was home to elements of III/JG5. These aircraft received a warning of approaching enemy aircraft and scrambled a dozen Bf109s and FW190s.

The formation leader, S/Ldr Barnes, gave the order to withdraw but it was too late, the German fighters were among them. What followed was a confusing series of dogfights between 3-4 aircraft. The first casualty was a Mustang from 315 Polish Squadron. F/O Andrzej Czerwiński (Mustang III HB857/C) was shot down in flames by a Bf109. The victor did not have time to relish his success however, as he was pounced on and shot down by F/Sgt Jakub Bargiełowski. This was Bargiełowski's fifth victory. A Messerschmitt attacked Bargiełowski from behind but F/Lt Wiza came to his rescue and shot the German down. Wiza claimed another Bf109 shot down during this combat. W/O Bolesław Czerwiński claimed one more. Two of the Focke-Wulfs were reported to have collided in mid air after trying to evade an attack from W/O Ryszard Idrian.

At the same time as this combat was taking place a number of Bf109s from 11./JG5, led by Oblt Rudi Glöckner, were attacking the Beaufighters from 144 and 404 Squadrons. A number of the aircraft were damaged in these attacks, while one from 404 Squadron, LZ448, had to ditch. It is possible *Gefr* Dieter Baasch shot down the Beaufighter. Another 404 Squadron aircraft, NT916, also suffered damage when an exploding shell hit the navigator's cupola. Splinters injured the navigator, W/O M H Michael.

It was now the turn of the Mosquitos to receive the attention of the German fighters. All four Tse-tse were attacked just after 1400hrs. Two of them, PZ301/T1 (F/O Woodcock/ F/O J J Vacher) and PZ252/Z1 (F/Lt Beattie/F/Lt E Gittens), were able to evade their attackers and escaped undamaged. One of the enemy fighters latched onto the tail of the Tse-tse being flown by F/Lt Beattie. F/O Woodcock saw this and rapidly changed course to bring his Tse-tse in behind the fighter. This in turn saved Woodcock as another enemy fighter had lined up on him. The fighter that was behind Beattie then made off. It was not the same story for the other two however. Both aircraft, NT225/O (F/O Cosman RCAF DFC/F/O Freedman) and PZ346/Z (F/O Wing RCAF/F/Sgt Shield, RAAF), were shot down with the loss of both crews. It is possible that Lt Podewils from 11/JG5 shot down one of these Mosquitos. He reported shooting down a Beaufighter at 1415hrs, but this could have been misidentified.

By 1420hrs it was all over, the remaining aircraft headed for home. A few of the Mosquitos and Beaufighters limped away on one engine. The Poles were credited with four enemy fighters destroyed with two more as probables. The German pilots claimed a total of 13 twin-engined aircraft and one single engine aircraft destroyed. These claims were grossly overestimated, as only two Tse-tse, one Beaufighter and one Mustang were lost. It could be that when the Beaufighters applied full throttle thick black smoke poured from the exhausts, making the Germans think they had inflicted severe damage and thereby claiming the aircraft as destroyed. With the loss of two Tse-tse it was decided that in future they would have escorting Mosquitos behind them to prevent a recurrence of the day's losses.

The *Luftwaffe* admitted to the loss of only two Bf109s. *Uffz* Harry Bernhardt, Bf109G6 *Werk.no* 410818 10/JG5 and *Uffz* Raimund Bruscagin, Bf109G6 *Werk.no* 410816 11/JG5. The *Luftwaffe* claimed this battle as a big success as the large formation of RAF aircraft was broken up and could not make a co-ordinated attack on the shipping.

Three days later on the 10th the Tse-tse were out again on an anti-shipping patrol to Flekkefjord. Two Tse-tse, MM425/L (F/O Woodcock/F/O Vacher) and NT224/E1 (F/O Hayton/F/O Day), were in company with five 248 Squadron FBVIs, six Mosquitos from

143 Squadron and 4 from 235 Squadron. It had been reported that a ship was stationary in the mouth of Flekkefjord and if sunk would block the fjord.

On reaching their patrol area they found that the ship was no longer there. Continuing their patrol they came across the German freighter *Gudrun*, 1,485t, lying at anchor near Kokodden Light House. Near her were the hospital ship *Pita* and the anti-submarine vessels *UJ1706*, *UJ1707* and *UJ1767* (1x37mm and 4x20mm). The *Gudrun* was carrying a cargo of cement and ammunition in the hold and drums of petrol on the deck. She had a gun platform at the bow and stern, each mounting a 20mm cannon. The 248 Squadron FBVIs went in first as flak suppression followed by the Tse-tse. F/O Hayton went in after the FBVIs and fired off four rounds of 6pdr claiming 2 dry hits and a possible third hit amidships. F/O Woodcock followed and also fired four rounds claiming three hits amidships. An explosion was seen and the ship burst into flames. *Signalobergefreite* R Kienley was seriously injured during the attack while *Kapitan* E Steinbrink, *Funker* G Dankelmann, Carpenter W Load and Seaman J Riske all suffered light wounds. At 1600hrs a motorboat came alongside and took off *Funker* Dankelmann and took him to a nearby hospital ship. With no power due to engine failure *Gudrun* was subsequently towed into shallow water near Abelnes by one of the escorts. The crew was successful in putting out the fires and saving the cargo of ammunition but the ship eventually sank. Flak was experienced from shore batteries as well as from the ships, although no aircraft were hit. Further vessels were spotted but none were attacked. An enemy aircraft thought to be a Fw190 was sighted but this dived to sea level and made off.

On the 12th the last Tse-tse, PZ468/Z, was delivered to the squadron. Two more Tse-tse, PZ469 and PZ470, were built but these were never delivered to an operational squadron, instead they went straight into storage.

During the night of the 15th a German convoy was passing Sognefjord when one of the ships, *Ferndale*, ran aground. Stuck fast, the other ships of the convoy sailed on leaving one escort vessel, *VP.5305* Jäger and a tug, *Fairplay X*. *VP.5305* was the ex-Norwegian whaler *Hval VI* that had been seized by the Germans and converted into an escort vessel. A salvage vessel, *Parat*, was ordered to assist the stricken vessel in any way it could.

In the morning of the 16th a mixed force of Mosquitos from 143, 235 and 248 Squadrons took off on a Rover patrol led by S/Ldr Maurice. Two Tse-tse, PZ252/Z1 (F/O Hayton/F/O

The Mosquitoes not only had to contend with shipboard AA but also from shore batteries as well. Here a 20mm gun prepares for action.
(Author's Collection)

51

FW190A-3 (White 7) from III/JG5 based at Herdla in 1945. In December 1944 III/JG5 moved to Southern Norway to combat the increasing attacks on the Norwegian convoys.

(Kjetil Åkra)

Day) and MM425/L (F/O Woodcock/F/O Vacher), were also part of the formation. Just after take off at an altitude of about 200ft the port propeller of MM425/L feathered itself then the engine revved up to 3,500rpm. The starboard undercarriage then failed to retract. Woodcock attempted to feather the port engine but it failed to do so. Unable to gain altitude to make a safe bale out Woodcock managed to coax the wallowing Mosquito back round to the airfield. Here he carried out a belly landing and both crew members were able to extract themselves from the aircraft without any difficulty. Due to the extensive damage caused by the crash it was impossible to carry out a functional test of the undercarriage. It was thought the engine problem might have been caused by sludging of the pilot valve in the constant speed unit (CSU). Failure may have been due to the sluggish action of the CSU. Again extensive damage caused by the crash landing prevented any functional tests to be carried out. The aircraft was declared a write off and was struck off charge the next day.

During the crossing of the North Sea S/Ldr Maurice was informed that a large vessel was aground at Krakhellsund. Swinging the formation round he brought them over the stricken *Ferndale*. The flak suppression Mosquitos went in first and raked the decks with 20mm and machine gun fire knocking out some AA positions and forcing other gun crews to take cover, in order to make it easier for the attacking aircraft. The *Ferndale* and *Parat* were severely damaged by both the Tse-tse and rocket firing Mosquitos with a number of casualties from both vessels. F/O Hayton carried out a number of passes and claimed 6 hits with his 6 pdr.

Return fire from the ships struck one of 248 Squadrons Mosquitos and the pilot carried out a successful ditching. Although both crewmembers escaped from their sinking aircraft they both died from exposure. A number of other aircraft received AA damage, but they all arrived safely back at base.

During the afternoon four Mosquitos from 248 Squadron and two from 235 Squadron carried out a second strike on the same vessels. Again two Tse-tse, PZ301/T1 (F/O Peacock/ F/O Field) and MM242/H (F/Lt A McLeod/ W/O H Wheeley), were involved. W/Cdr Sise led the aircraft in on a stern attack, causing further damage, which finally sank both vessels. A total of 7 hits were claimed by the Tse-tse. On board the *Ferndale* three of the German flak gunners, *Matrosenobergefreiters* Walter Kutcher, Artur Spandehra and Konrad Watzlawik, died in the attacks. Accurate AA fire from *VP.5305* struck a Mosquito from 235 Squadron and it crashed with the loss of F/Lt K Beruldsen and his navigator. Another Mosquito was hit in the engine and flew back to Banff on one engine. As it came into land it veered off the runway and crashed, both crewmembers were able to escape relatively unharmed.

In the early hours of Boxing Day a reconnaissance Mosquito had spotted two ships in Leirvik harbour. A strike was laid on using aircraft from Banff and Dallachy. S/Ldr Jackson-Smith DFC led off 12 Mosquitos, including 2 Tse-tse, PZ301/T1 (F/O Peacock/F/O Field) and PZ252/Z1 (F/O Hayton/F/O Day), and 2 FB VIs from 248 Squadron low over the North Sea towards Leirvik. Making landfall at 1334hrs the formation approached Leirvik Harbour where the two vessels were spotted. The Tse-tse went in and opened fire on the *Cygnus* and *Tenerife*, as did the rocket firing Mosquitos. On board the *Cygnus* engineer *Oddmar* Jens Klepp was killed and the vessel was left in flames. The *Tenerife* was also hit hard and was last seen billowing smoke. Both of these vessels were later repaired and returned to service.

Return fire was heavy, not only from the vessels but also from the shore batteries with their heavier 88mm AA guns. Some of the Mosquitos received minor AA damage. The other danger faced by the strike force was the presence of German fighters. A mixed force of Bf109s and Fw190s from 16/JG5 arrived over the harbour. A number of individual dogfights took place and Uffz Halstrick claimed one of the Mosquitos

shot down, although a Bf109 was claimed in return. No German fighters were lost on this occasion. During this dogfight F/O Hayton (PZ252/Z1) fired his Molins gun at a formation of enemy fighters. It is not known if he actually hit any of them.

Two days later S/Ldr Orreck (248 Squadron) led off 2 FBVIs and two Tse-tse, MM424/H (F/O Woodcock/F/O Vacher) and NT224/E1 (F/Lt Beattie/F/Lt Gittens), in formation with four aircraft each from 143 and 235 Squadrons. As they approached the Norwegian coast they encountered four vessels travelling in line astern and doing about 6-8 knots. On sighting the aircraft the vessels increased speed and started to circle and fire off an intensive flak barrage. The formation continued on its way and off Skudeneshavn they found a stationary vessel. This was the 616t *La France*, which had arrived a few weeks earlier for repairs. The Mosquitos duly attacked and numerous hits were achieved with 20mm, RPs and 6 pdr. The vessel, which was emitting smoke, was left low in the water and it eventually capsized. F/O Woodcock also attacked an AA battery and scored a number of hits, which silenced it.

JANUARY 1945

Three Tse-tse, PZ468/Z (F/Lt McLeod/W/O Wheeley), PZ301/T1 (F/O Peacock/F/O Field) and NT224/E1 (F/O Woodcock/F/O Vacher), took part in a strike against the *Claus Rickmers* (5,165t) on the 9th January. This vessel had already been damaged during a previous strike on the 7th. W/Cdr Maurice led 15 Mosquitos to Leirvik harbour where the *Claus Rickmers* was holed up. In the harbour were a total of six merchant vessels and six escort vessels, including *VP.5304 Seehund*, *VP.5308 O B Rogge* and Raumboot *R63*. Due to the increasing presence of German fighters the Mosquitos received an escort of 15 Mustangs from 315 Polish Squadron.

As the formation came over the target the pilots jockeyed for position and commenced the attack. F/O Woodcock saw his shells hit the stern of the *Claus Rickmers*. He then attacked an AA position, which had just opened fire. After firing half a dozen rounds from his Molins gun the AA position fell silent. Numerous rockets hit the *Claus Rickmers* above and below the waterline and a number of fires broke out. One of the escort vessels, *VP.5304* was also hit and damaged during the attack. AA gunners claimed three of the attackers shot down and several more damaged. None of the Mosquitos were lost, although a number were damaged. It could be that the German gunners had seen the large muzzle flash from the Tse-tse's Molins guns and assumed that the aircraft had exploded, thus claiming the aircraft as destroyed. Hits were also claimed on a further merchant vessel and two more escorts.

A Bf109G from III/JG5 based at Gossen. The Banff Strike Wing suffered a number of losses from the Gossen based fighters.
(Kjetil Åkra)

P47 was the Dutch submarine Dolfjin, *which was attacked by mistake by two Tse-tse on 10th January 1945. No one was injured and the submarine suffered light damage.*

(Adrian Walsh)

The next day a number of Mosquitos were instructed to carry out a Rover patrol between Bergen and Haugesund. Included in the formation were Tse-tse PZ301/T1 (F/Lt McLeod/W/O Wheeley) and NT224/E1 (F/Lt J G Cooper/F/Lt G L P Palombi) from 248 Squadron. As they approached the Inner Roads a surfaced U-boat was spotted. Four of the Mosquitos approached from the beam but were spotted by the crew. The submarine crash-dived but not before it was hit by 20mm and machine gun fire. On returning to base the crews were informed of the identity of their target. It turned out that the U-boat was actually the Dutch submarine *Dolfijn*, from the 9th Submarine Flotilla based at Dundee in Scotland, which was carrying out trials after being repaired. The *Dolfijn* suffered damage to the conning tower, periscope and aerial array.

A Tse-tse was in action again on the 11th. Another mixed formation of 13 Mosquitos from Banff, including PZ468/Z (F/O Peacock/F/O Field) and 21 Beaufighters from Dallachy, carried out an armed strike towards Flekkefjord. As they neared the target the German defences sprang into action. From the north came a formation of 6 Bf109s and Fw190s from JG5, which had taken off from their base. Further German fighters from 14/JG5 took off from Lister and attacked from the south. On spotting the German fighters the slower Beaufighters turned about and headed for home. A few were caught and one of them was shot down. The Mosquitos, being faster and more agile, turned into the enemy fighters. During the dogfight that followed one of the Mosquitos was lost. Three enemy fighters were claimed shot down. F/Lt Russel from 235 Squadron claimed one of the fighters shot down. F/O Peacock attacked one of the Fw190s from the port quarter. In a very tight turn and at a range of 300yds he fired four 6pdr rounds at the enemy fighter. No hits were registered but it must have scared the enemy pilot witless.

Actual German losses were *Uffz* Klemens Kohler, Bf109G6 *Werk.no* 462503 14/JG5 and *Uffz* Werner Nieft, Bf109G6 *Werk.no* 464816 14/JG5.

On 15th January 1945 a mixed formation of Mosquito FB VIs and Tse-tse attacked the Claus Rickmers at Leirvik Harbour. Here we see one of the escorting vessels being narrowly missed by a salvo of rockets.

(Andy Bird)

The Tse-tse were involved in another strike against the *Claus Rickmers* on the 15th. This would be the third attack on this vessel, which was rumoured to be carrying heavy water, a vital commodity for the German atomic bomb programme. Four Tse-tse took part in this operation. They were:

NT224/E1   F/Lt Cooper/F/Lt Palombi
PZ252/Z1   F/O Peacock/F/O Field
PZ300/S1   F/O Woodcock/F/O Vacher
PZ468/Z   F/Lt McLeod/W/O Wheeley

Ahead of the formation flew two Mosquitos from 333 Squadron, which were to act as scouts for the main formation. Flying through virtually zero visibility and frequent snow showers the aircraft searched through various inlets and islands along the way. As they approached Leirvik they came under intense AA fire, which struck one of the Mosquitos causing it to blow up in mid air, there were no survivors.

As the main formation reached Leirvik the AA fire increased and, with alarm bells ringing, the defending German fighters roared into the air from Herdla and headed south. The anti-flak Mosquitos dived across the harbour followed by the main strike aircraft. Reeling under a salvo of rockets the escort vessel *VP.5304 Seehund* quickly sank. Two other vessels, *VP.5308 O B Rogge* and *Raumboot R63* were also damaged. The *Claus Rickmers* was also hit yet again, but the vessel was already resting on the bottom next to the quay. Several of the Mosquitos were damaged and one of them, from 235 Squadron, was shot down. As the Mosquitos completed their attack and reformed for the flight home the enemy fighters, identified as Fw190s, appeared.

S/Ldr Fitch, 143 Squadron, had his Mosquito raked by cannon and machine gun fire. Over the radio there were cries for help as a lot of confused dogfights took place in and out of the murky conditions. One Mosquito was being attack by a Fw190 when a Tse-tse, flown by F/O Peacock, came in behind the German fighter and fired off a number of rounds from his Molins gun. The Focke Wulf broke off the attack and headed inland. It would appear that this aircraft actually crash-landed and the pilot was rescued by two Norwegians, only to die of his injuries in hospital. It is possible that Peacock's victim was *Uffz* Oskar Helbing, flying an Fw190A-3 *Werk.no* 2172 "White 14" from 9./JG5. As Peacock did not see his victim crash he did not file a claim for it.

The usual mount of W/O Sztramko, Mustang KH485 PK-R, is seen accompanied by what appears to be PK-Q (probably FB155, often flown by F/O Bibrowicz). Note dorsal fin and absence of white band behind the spinner of KH485.
(via Wilhelm Ratuszyński)

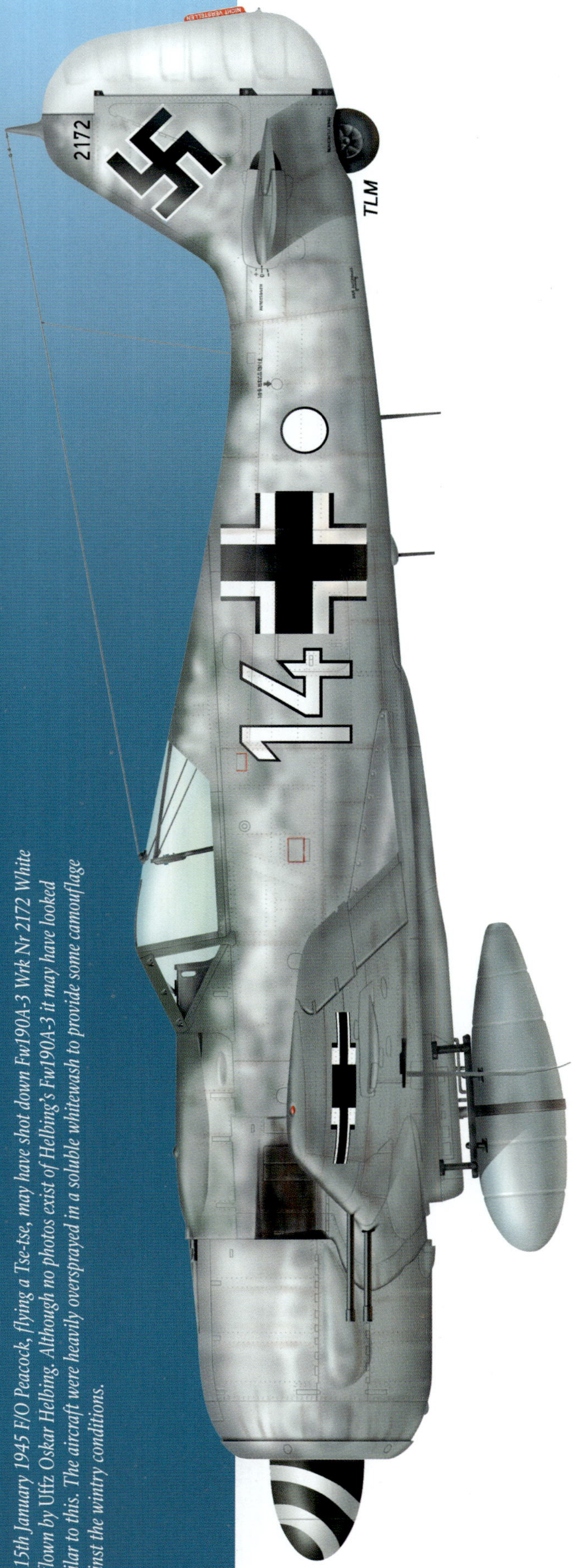

On 15th January 1945 F/O Peacock, flying a Tse-tse, may have shot down Fw190A-3 Wrk Nr 2172 White 14 flown by Uffz Oskar Helbing. Although no photos exist of Helbing's Fw190A-3 it may have looked similar to this. The aircraft were heavily oversprayed in a soluble whitewash to provide some camouflage against the wintry conditions.

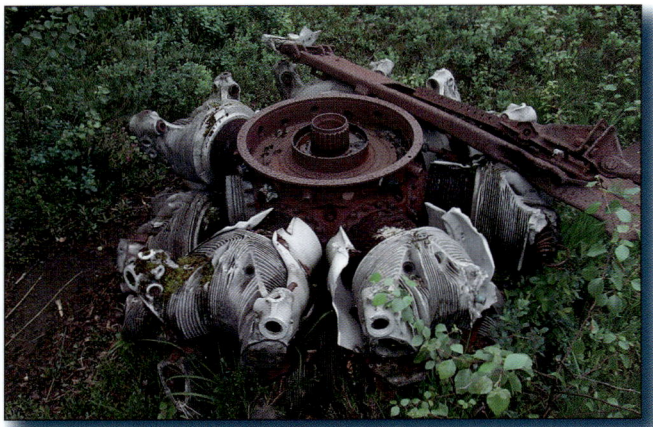

Very little remains of Uffz Helbing's Fw190. Here is the BMW engine. **(Kjell Sørensen)**

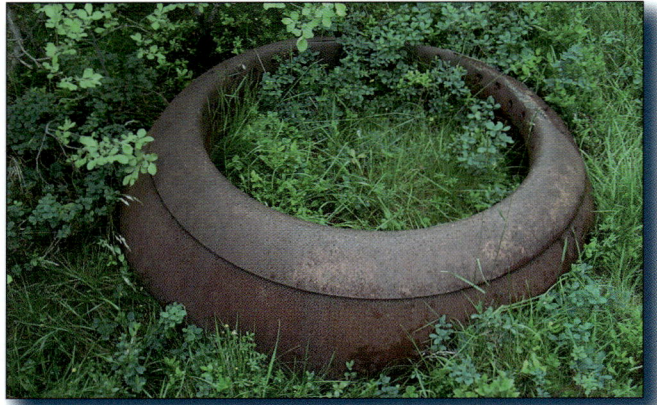

The armoured cowling ring of Helbing's FW190. **(Kjell Sørensen)**

The German fighters claimed four of the Mosquitos shot down. Two other German fighters, also from 9/JG5, were lost in this combat. *Uffz* Richard Lehnert Fw190A8 *Werk.no* 350183 "White 16" and *Uffz* Waldow Zeuner Fw190A8 *Werk.no* 737410 "White 4".

Claus Rickmers was captured by the Allies at Bergen, and after being repaired was placed in British service as the *Empire Carron* in 1947.

This was to be the last combat operation for the Tse-tse with 248 Squadron and the Banff Strike Wing. Although removed from operational flying the aircraft remained at Banff for some weeks. They were involved in the training of pilots for the FB VIs. As such they undertook air to air, air to sea and circuit flights. This was not the end of operations for the Tse-tse, as a new role had been found for them.

A new lease of life

During the early months of 1945 there had been an increase in the number of midget submarine attacks on shipping that was supplying the invasion forces in Europe. As the Tse-tse was a specialist anti-submarine hunter it was decided to transfer them to the south east coast of England to undertake anti-submarine patrols off the Dutch and German coasts. Therefore in mid-March the whole of 'C' Flight was posted to 254 Squadron at North Coates under the command of F/O Woodcock.

NORTH COATES

In 1942 Coastal Command had formed the first Strike Wing at North Coates. One of the first squadrons in this wing was 254 Squadron equipped with Beaufighters. Now almost three years later 254 Squadron was still at North Coates and still equipped with Beaufighters. A total of four Tse-tse (HX904, MM424, PZ252 and PZ301) were transferred to 254 Squadron on 16th March. Two of these (HX904 and MM424) were sent to Bircham Newton for overhaul, within a few days. HX904 returned on the 29th April and MM424 on the 16th May. Two more Tse-tse (PZ300 and PZ468) arrived on the 21st March while the last one (NT224) didn't arrived until 16th May. From here the Tse-tse would carry out operations, mainly against U-Boats, until the end of the War.

APRIL

By the beginning of April four Tse-tse (PZ252, PZ300, PZ301 and PZ468) were available for operations. The first strike by the Tse-tse was carried out on the 3rd of April. Two Tse-tse, PZ301/QM-B (F/O Woodcock/F/O Vacher) and PZ468/QM-D (F/O Hayton/F/O Day), were part of an anti-shipping strike set for the Borkum area. They were accompanied by 6 torpedo equipped Beaufighters (Torbeaus) and 3 anti-flak Beaufighters, all from 254 Squadron. W/Cdr Cartridge led this formation and they were tasked to attack any shipping reported in the area by the Tactical Air Force aircraft, which were flying ahead of the formation. A convoy of three ships was sighted and they were identified as Swedish relief ships, so no attack was carried out. Nothing further was seen and the formation headed for home.

The next strike for the Tse-tse was on the 12th. PZ301/QM-B (F/Lt A E Richardson/F/O A F Godwin) took off at 1442hrs on an anti-midget submarine patrol. A radio message informed Richardson that there was a target at position 52°12'N 03°12'E. Fifteen minutes later a second message stated that the target had been sunk. On hearing this Richardson set course for base.

Fifty-five minutes after Richardson had taken off PZ300/QM-A (F/O R A Davis/ W/O W Buckley) lifted off from North Coates on a similar patrol. After almost an hour into the patrol Davis sighted the conning tower and stern of a U-boat, which he identified as a Biber. Davis carried out six attacks and thought that he hit the Biber once during the second attack and twice during the third attack. A Wellington from 524 Squadron arrived on the scene and dropped two depth

The Tse-tse that served with 254 Squadron received full squadron codes. PZ468 was coded QM-D. The D-Day stripes have been overpainted and the spinners are sky with a white band.

charges and attacked with cannon. The depth charges were seen to overshoot by about 30ft, but hits were achieved with the cannon. Davis made further attacks until he had exhausted his 6pdr ammunition. The Biber had by now disappeared and all that was left were several pieces of wreckage. Davis continued with his patrol and landed back at base at 1927hrs.

254 Squadron flew numerous patrols the next day. Tse-tse PZ301/QM-B (F/Lt Richardson/F/O Godwin) was off at 1434hrs. Two hours into the patrol the Tse-tse was approached by two P-47 Thunderbolts which appeared to be getting ready to attack. After the Tse-tse fired off the correct recognition signals the Thunderbolts made off. At 1639hrs Richardson saw what he thought was a U-boat's snorkel and fired off three rounds at it. A closer inspection showed it to be a marine marker. A further round was fired at a silver coloured object, which was a near miss. A little later Richardson fired five rounds at a black and white striped pole, which he thought was a periscope.

At 1539hrs Tse-tse PZ300/QM-A (Plt Off A W Ellis/Plt Off L Rice) took off on patrol. Nothing of any importance was sighted and the Mosquito landed back at North Coates at 1925hrs.

On the 14th two Tse-tse PZ300/QM-A (F/O Davis/W/O Buckley) and PZ252/QM-C (F/O Hayton/F/O Day) carried out separate patrols but no enemy vessels were sighted. On the 16th Tse-tse PZ300/QM-A (Plt Off Ellis/Plt Off Rice) had to abort a patrol early due to low cloud. Tse-tse PZ468/QM-D (F/Lt Richardson/W/O N Jones) had slightly better luck with a patrol later in the day. They sighted the smoke and wake from a snorkel and carried out an attack. Two 6pdr rounds were fired but the result were not observed. Further patrols continued the next day. Tse-tse PZ252/QM-C (F/O Davis/W/O Buckley) and PZ468/QM-D (F/O Hayton/F/O Day) each carried out one patrol but nothing was seen.

On the 18th Tse-tse PZ252/QM-C (Plt Off Ellis/Plt Off Rice) and PZ468/QM-D (F/Lt Richardson/W/O Jones) in company with two aircraft from 236 Squadron carried out an armed reconnaissance. At 2004hrs four barges were spotted to the west of Langeooge but were not attacked. Twenty minutes later a group of five surface craft were spotted. As Richardson passed over them he realised they were U-boats, possibly type XXIII. One had already dived and he pulled round and opened fire on one of them. He was only able to get off two rounds, which were near misses, before the U-boat dived. The formation continued on with the patrol and although no further enemy vessels were sighted they suffered some accurate AA fire from Ameland and Terschelling.

On the 20th Tse-tse PZ468/QM-D (F/O Hayton/F/O Day) carried out an armed reconnaissance but nothing was sighted. The next day it was the turn of Tse-tse PZ300/QM-A (F/O Woodcock/F/O Vacher) and PZ468/QM-D (F/Lt Richardson/F/O Godwin) but as with the day before it was another fruitless patrol. On the 24th Tse-tse PZ300/QM-A (Plt Off Ellis/Plt Off Rice) was on patrol in the Bight area when Ellis thought he saw a periscope. He came into attack and fired off two rounds from his 6pdr. Coming in for another attack he

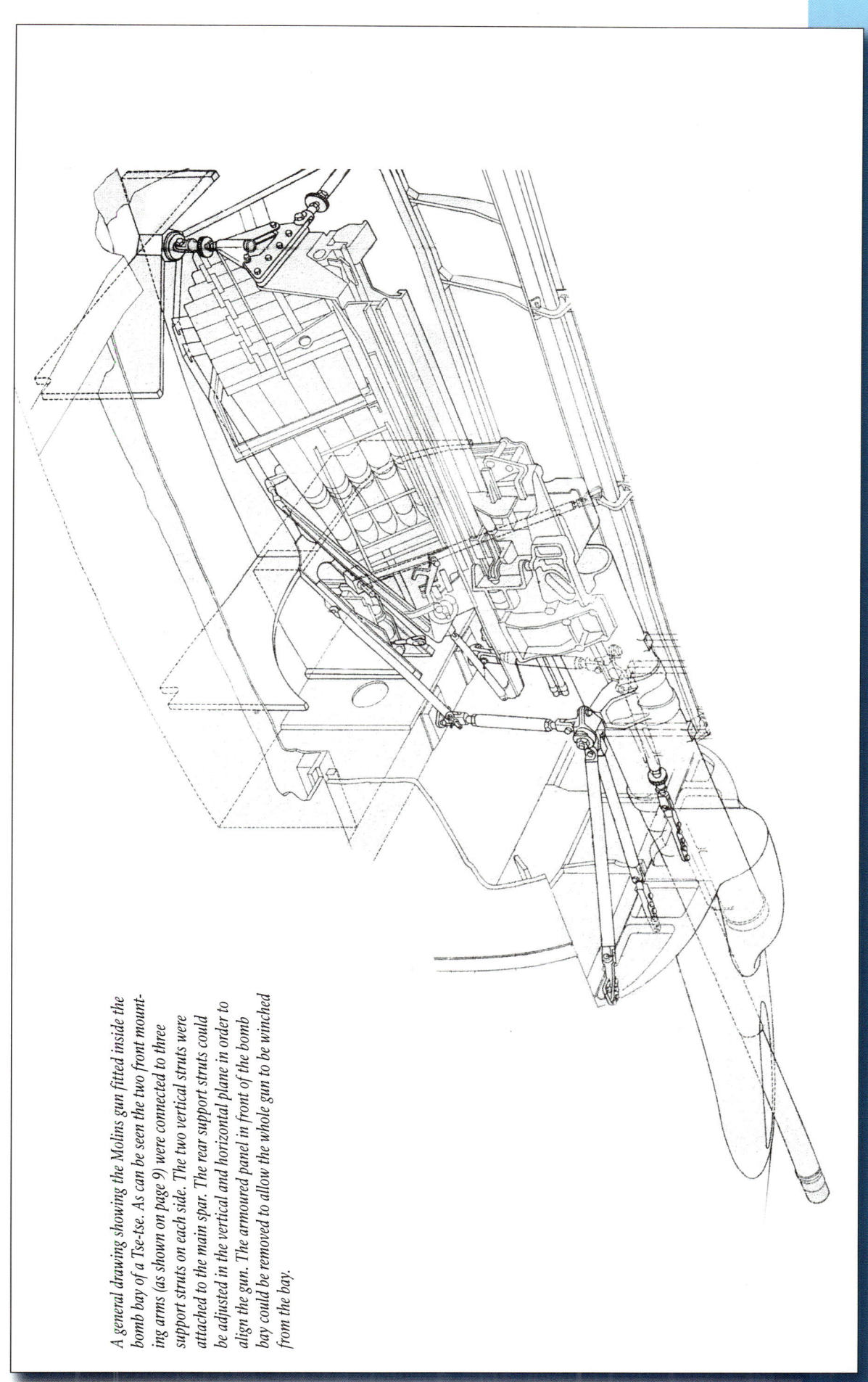

A general drawing showing the Molins gun fitted inside the bomb bay of a Tse-tse. As can be seen the two front mounting arms (as shown on page 9) were connected to three support struts on each side. The two vertical struts were attached to the main spar. The rear support struts could be adjusted in the vertical and horizontal plane in order to align the gun. The armoured panel in front of the bomb bay could be removed to allow the whole gun to be winched from the bay.

saw that the 'periscope' was actually a conical buoy with a staff attached to it. The next day Tse-tse PZ300/QM-A (F/Lt Richardson/F/O Godwin) undertook an armed patrol. A number of fishing vessels were spotted off Cuxhaven and these were left alone. Another patrol by Tse-tse PZ468/QM-D (F/O Hayton/F/O Day) was cut short due to engine problems. The aircraft returned to base safely.

The last Tse-tse sortie of the month was undertaken by PZ300/QM-A (Plt Off Ellis/Plt Off Rice) and PZ468/QM-D (F/Lt Richardson/F/O Godwin) on the 26th. They carried out a joint armed reconnaissance. Apart from sighting 15-20 fishing vessels their patrol was fruitless.

At some point towards the end of April PZ252/QM-C suffered some damage, whether from enemy action or an accident in unclear. The aircraft was repaired on site by a team from de Havilland and was eventually returned to service on 10th May. Although HX904 arrived at the squadron on the 29th April it does not appear to have taken part in any operations before the end of the War. This would leave just three Tse-tse to take part in operations during May. These were PZ300/QM-A, PZ301/QM-B and PZ468/QM-D.

MAY

On the 2nd May two Tse-tse, PZ300/QM-A (F/Lt Davis/W/O Buckley) and PZ468/QM-D (F/O J M Hayton/F/O C H Day) carried out an anti-U-boat sortie but nothing was spotted. Both aircraft returned to base. In the morning of the 3rd two Tse-tse, PZ301/QM-B (Plt Off Ellis/Plt Off Rice) and PZ468/QM-D (F/O Hayton/F/O Day), took off on an armed patrol. When they reached position 53°37'N 06°36'E they spotted a U-boat travelling on the surface. Ellis attacked first and fired 6 rounds, followed by Hayton who also fired 6 rounds. It was thought at least 7 rounds landed close to the submarine. A large spout of water about 40-50ft high was seen. This may have been caused by the submarine crash diving and venting its tanks. It is possible this submarine was *U-2336*. On the 7th May this U-boat entered the Firth of Forth in Scotland and sank two freighters. These were the last merchant ships to be sunk by a U-boat during WWII.

Later in the evening of the 3rd Tse-tse PZ300/QM-A (F/Lt Davis/W/O Buckley) took off on an armed patrol. Nothing was seen and the aircraft returned to base. On landing the port tyre burst and the aircraft swung to port. This was too much strain for the undercarriage which collapsed. The Mosquito was eventually repaired but never returned to operational service. It was struck off charge in December 1945.

At 1005 hrs on the 4th Tse-tse PZ301/QM-B (F/O Ellis/Plt Off Rice) took off on a lone armed reconnaissance. In the patrol area smoke was seen and on going to investigate they found a small barge burning furiously. Nothing else was spotted and they returned to base.

The last operational sortie by a Tse-tse was carried in the early evening. Two Tse-tse, PZ301/QM-B (F/O Hayton/F/O Vacher) and PZ468/QM-D (F/O Davis/W/O Buckley), took off at 1635hrs. They were to be used as outriders for the Dallachy Strike wing. Their mission was to radio the main force of any enemy shipping they sighted. At 1835hrs they sighted 3 small merchant vessels with 2 escorts. Due to problems with their radio they failed to make contact with the main force. About 10 minutes later they came across another small convoy. Again they failed to contact the main force so F/O Hayton attacked one of the ships. He fired 6 rounds and saw a number of explosions on the stern of the ship. A white flag was hoisted and he broke off the attack.

At 1859hrs and 1908hrs further ships were sighted but they were still unable to raise the main force. When a lone ship was spotted at 1914hrs both Tse-tse attacked. A total of 11 wet and dry hits were claimed on the ship, which was estimated at 2,500t. Two minutes later both aircraft broke off the attack and headed for base, landing at 2055hrs.

PZ301/QM-B was damaged on the 5th May and repaired on site by de Havilland. The aircraft returned to service in June.

With the war in Europe now over most of the aircraft were stood down from operations. The Tse-tse remained with 254 Squadron for a few more months. On 5th July W/O J T Madsen went up on his first solo in a Tse-tse, HX904. After a 40-minute flight Madsen came into land. On touch down the Mosquito swung on landing and the undercarriage collapsed. The Mosquito was classed as category 'AC', but was later reclassed as category 'E' and struck off charge on the 30th. On the 17th July MM242 suffered damaged in a flying accident. The aircraft was repaired on site by 67 Maintenance Unit and returned to service in August.

The Tse-tse were eventually retired from front line service and passed on to 9 and 10 Maintenance Units. Here they lingered on for over a year before being struck off charge in late 1946.

Tse-tse PZ468 later served with 254 Squadron, as seen here. The aircraft received the codes QM-D. The nose cone appears to be darker and suggests that the original has been replaced, probably due to combat damage.

(Andy Bird)

The Type XXIII U-boat was a coastal submarine, which began to enter service in June 1944. It's possible that one of these, U-2336 was attacked by a 254 Squadron Tse-tse on 3rd March 1945.

With the success of the Coastal Command Tse-tse the US Navy became interested in heavy calibre anti-shipping weapons. In April 1945 one of the Tse-tse Mosquitos, PZ467, was shipped to the United States for evaluation.

PZ467 was built at Hatfield in October 1944 and was accepted into the RAF in November. Here it went straight to 27 MU at Shawbury in December for modifications. The aircraft never saw active service with a front line squadron and as such it ended up at RAF Pershore in March. From here it was prepared ready for shipping to the USA.

The aircraft arrived at Dorval, Quebec in Canada from where it was ferried to Petuxant River Naval Air Station, Maryland in 30 April 1945. The aircraft received the Bureau number 91106. The Mosquito was part of a programme to evaluate large calibre weapons fitted to aircraft. A B25H also took part in the trials. These trials were commanded by Commander, later Rear Admiral, Albert R Matter. The engineering officer was Lt (jg) Walter W Deschler.

A number of test flights were made against a floating target anchored in Chesapeake Bay. Deschler flew in several of these flights as an observer. He later commented that during a continuous burst of cannon fire the Mosquito hesitated in the air due to the recoil of the 57mm gun. During the landing of one of these flights, the pilot misjudged the angle of descent and speed of approach. The Mosquito suffered a hard landing, which caused damage to the undercarriage units. While waiting for the repairs to be carried out the Molins gun was removed from the aircraft for use in ground trials. After the trials had been completed the Mosquito was transferred to the War Assets Corporation for disposal and was placed in storage at Augusta, Georgia.

This was not the end for the Mosquito, far from it. Ex-air force Mosquitos were much sought after by civilians, companies and foreign air forces the world over. It was to have a number of civilian owners over the next 2 years. The first owner was Allison Perry, an ex-Air Transport Command pilot, who owned his own aircraft brokerage business. He purchased the Mosquito in 1946 with plans to enter it in the Bendix Air Race. The aircraft was registered NX66422 and was painted grey overall with red spinners. While ferrying the aircraft to Lake Wales, Florida, it ground looped on landing, inflicting damage to one of the undercarriage units. This brought an end to Perry's notion of entering the Bendix Air Race and he put the Mosquito up for sale.

The next interested party was Marvin Dunlay from Birmingham, Alabama. An ex-RAF pilot with the Air Transport Auxiliary, Marvin had ferried many Mosquitos around the world during WWII. After an inspection of the Mosquito in Florida, still with the bent undercarriage, Marvin purchased the aircraft. He kept it for about a year before advertising it for sale.

Carlo De Ponti, who acted as a sales agent for Lt Col Al K Rozawick, bought the Mosquito. Al Rozawick owned the World Air Shows and was an ex-Air Transport Command pilot. It would appear that the Mosquito was put up for sale again not long after it was purchased by De Ponti.

The Mosquito's last owner was Maj Jean P Doar from Charlotte, North Carolina. Doar was a former fighter pilot with the 13th Air Force in the Pacific. During a reconnaissance mission his engine failed and he had to ditch in the ocean some 200 miles from Guadalcanal. He was rescued six hours later. Volunteering for a second tour he was assigned to the 8th Fighter Squadron, Chinese-American Composite Wing, 14th Air Force. His Mustang was hit by AA fire and shot down on the 2 August during an attack on Hangkow. He was posted as missing in action until he returned six weeks later having been rescued by Chinese Communist troops.

After the War Jean became interested in air racing and even planned to challenge Bill Odom's around the world speed record. Browsing through the advertisements in Trade-A-Plane Jean spotted the Mosquito, NX66422, that was up for sale. After making contact with De Ponti Jean bought the Mosquito for $5,000. The aircraft was flown to Charlotte on the 20 September 1947. The task of modifying the airframe for the around the world speed record began almost immediately. For the next four months all the internal and external armour plating was removed. A large fuel tank was fitted in the bomb bay to increase the range. Full radio equipment was also fitted. At this time the aircraft was re-sprayed silver with red spinners and engine cowling. The legend 'The Silver Streak' was painted, probably in red, on the fuselage side.

To finance the trip Jean set up 'Around the World, Inc' and planned to sell shares at $100 each. To launch this fund-raising a demonstration flight was laid on for 27 January 1948. At 2.30pm the Mosquito taxied out and took off. After a couple of minutes into the flight the roof hatch blew open and the aircraft returned to the airport to carry out an emergency landing. As the aircraft touched down it swerved to starboard. Jean tried to counter this by applying the port brake. This caused the Mosquito to swerve to port and this was too much for the starboard undercarriage, which collapsed. The resulting ground loop inflicted major

View of the nose of PZ467 after its arrival in the US. The machine guns were removed in the UK and the ports blanked off.

(Pierre Babin)

Tse-tse PZ467 never saw operational service. It was destined to go to America for testing at the Patuxant River Naval Air Station in Maryland.

Port and starboard views of PZ467 in US markings. These are speculative as no known photos exists of the aircraft in US markings. Inset. A close up of the nose with the AT-28 code. The reason for this marking in unclear. The number 28 was applied under the nose.

Side view of the Silver Streak after all the modifications had been carried out for the around the World speed record.

(above byNorman Malayney)
(left by Ray Sturtivant)

For his World record attempt Jean Doar had the aircraft sprayed silver overall with red engine cowlings. The registration was in black, while the legend 'The de Havilland Mosquito' and "The Silver Streak' were in red.

damage to the starboard wing, engine and propeller. The airframe was beyond repair and this put an end to Jean's record attempt. The aircraft was pushed off the runway and later given to the airport fire department to use for training exercises. Before this however, Jean stripped off the two Merlin engines and sold them for $400 to someone in Miami who wanted them for his racing boat.

So ends the story of the last surviving Tse-tse. With so few aircraft converted into Tse-tse it's understandable that there are none left. All we have left of these aircraft are the fading memories of those who flew them and a few photographs. Not much of an epitaph for an aircraft that wrought havoc on enemy U-boats and shipping. Perhaps somewhere in Miami there is a boat still powered by a Tse-tse's Merlins.

A sorry looking Silver Streak sits on the runway after swerving on landing.
(Norman Malayney)

Jean Doar (right) during the pre-flight publicity shots for the demonstration flight on 27th January 1948.
(Norman Malayney)

Colours and markings

From the available evidence the Tse-tse were all camouflaged in the standard night fighter scheme of overall Medium Sea Grey with a Dark Green disruptive pattern on the upper surface of the wings, fuselage and tail. 36" Type 'C1' roundels were placed on the fuselage 54" from the trailing edge of the wing to the centre of the roundel. 54" Type 'B' roundels were applied to the upper wing 18ft from the centre line of the fuselage to the centre of the roundel. There was a 1" gap between the edge of the roundel and the aileron. Black 8" serial numbers were placed equidistant between the top and bottom of the fuselage and 6" in front of the tail plane. A 24" x 24" fin flash was placed on the fin. The Red and Blue segments were 11" wide and the White segment was 2" wide. The flash sat at the bottom of the fin with the Blue segment next to the rudder hinge line. Spinners were painted Sky, although this may have changed at a latter date to Medium Sea Grey. In January 1945 the upper wing roundels were changed to Type 'C' roundels. Propeller blades were Black with 4" Yellow tips.

While in squadron service the Tse-tse wore individual identification letters. These were usually Dull Red and may have had a White or Yellow outline. There is no evidence of the aircraft wearing full squadron codes while in service with 618 Squadron Special Detachment or 248 Squadron. During their service with 254 Squadron the Tse-tse wore the full squadron codes 'QM' followed by the individual letter. These codes were Black and had no outline. Individual letters used by the Tse-tse with 618 Squadron Special Detachment and 248 Squadron were E, E1, H, I, L, O, S1, T1, Z and Z1. The use of the number 1 after the letter signifies that there was already an aircraft in the Squadron with that letter in use, so the number 1 was applied after the letter to distinguish the two aircraft. It has often been stated that these numbered letters were used to distinguish the Tse-tse from the FBVIs. This is not the case. Full codes used by 254 Squadron were QM-A, QM-B, QM-C and QM-D. Others may have been used but these have not yet been identified.

Appendixes

APPENDIX 1

Tse-tse memories

F/O A H 'Hilly' Hilliard, pilot 618 Squadron

'The Mk XVIII Mosquito was heavier than the MkVI by some 1,600lbs – weight of the Molins gun, with a recoil force of 800lbs when fired, was within the limits of stress for the aircraft. When the gun was fired it was noticed that the instruments in the cockpit went to zero!

The Tse-tse had a tendency to swing to port on take-off; this was overcome by a little extra throttle on that engine to obtain a perfect lift off at about 180mph and a steady climb with +7lb boost at 170mph with the Merlin 25 engines.

The aircraft was a dream to fly. All controls operated at the 'touch of a button' so to speak. It was steady in a dive; stalling speed was 130mph, no power, undercarriage and flaps up. It did so very gently after the initial vibration.'

F/O Des Curtis, DFC, navigator 618 Squadron

'The first time we fired the gun was electrifying. The noise was deafening, the flame that accompanied the shell from the barrel enveloped the aircraft, and there was a robust jolt as the shell set off towards the target. The jolt was, in fact, the aircraft being propelled backwards for a microsecond by the recoil of the gun. The proof of this was demonstrated on one occasion, when we were returning as the leader in formation with Mosquito escorts after an uneventful patrol. We decided to fire a series of shots in level flight at normal cruising. None of the pilots in the formation adjusted throttles, yet very quickly we were overtaken by the aircraft on our port and starboard.

The second surprise was the clanging thuds below our armour-plated seats as the breechblock withdrew the spent cartridge and rammed home the next live round. The nearest equivalent to that sensation was that of an anti-aircraft shell exploding just below the aircraft, sending shrapnel clanging into the steel plates.'

F/Lt S B L Beattie, pilot 248 Squadron

'We normally crossed the North Sea (from Banff) at a couple of hundred feet to keep under the enemy radar, but later we climbed to 3,000 feet. On sighting the target we peeled off, straightened out at around 2,500 feet and then dived at the target. When we (the Tse-tse pilots) were aimed at the target we called out: 'Salvo, Salvo' over the VHF at which any of the others this side of the target would know to pull up and away as we then opened up with the M-gun.'

Vince Hawman engine fitter, 618 Squadron

'I managed to have a test firing flight with, I think, F/Lt Turner. Not being aircrew, I was thrilled to bits to be diving steeply at the sea. The aircraft seemed to stop momentarily and flames flashed over the windscreen every time he fired. I forget how many shells the magazine held but there was a stoppage near the end much to the chagrin of the pilot. The only damage I remember was when an enemy shell went through the nose cone just missing the gun barrel and out through an inspection panel. A fraction of a second later and it would have gone through the cockpit. We lost one aircraft and crew through an accident when two collided in mid-air, the other landing safely but damaged.'

APPENDIX 2

The Aircraft

A total of 17 Mosquito Mk VIs were converted into Mk XVIII Tse-tse. Below is a potted history of each aircraft as taken from the aircraft movement cards held by the Air Historical Branch. The number of operational sorties each aircraft carried out is in brackets. This has been taken from the various Squadron ORBs and does not include training missions.

HJ732 (Prototype)

Retained at Aircraft and Armament Experimental Establishment (A&AEE) undergoing various trials. In August 1943 it suffered an accident and was repaired by a team from de Havilland, Hatfield. Transferred to 10 Maintenance Unit in July 1945 and struck off charge in May 1946.

HX902 (2)

05/09/43	A&AEE
23/10/43	Delivered to 618 Squadron Special Detachment (SD). Coded 'O'.
04/11/43	Lost during attack on trawler. S/Ldr Rose/Sgt Cowley lost.

HX903 (30)

06/10/43	A&AEE
03/11/43	Delivered to 618 Squadron SD. Coded 'I'.
15/03/44	Suffered damage and repaired by team from de Havilland, Hatfield.
23/05/44	Transferred to 248 Squadron.
10/06/44	Lost in collision with Mosquito HR138. F/O Bonnet/F/O McNicol lost.

HX904 (26)

06/10/43	A&AEE
23/10/43	618 Squadron SD. Coded 'E'.
23/11/43	De Havilland, Hatfield. Possibly for repair due to damage received.
02/01/44	Category 'B' damage. Repaired at squadron level.
10/03/44	Category 'B' damage. Repaired off site at de Havilland, Hatfield.
08/05/44	Damaged and repaired on site.
23/05/44	Transferred to 248 Squadron.
22/11/44	Damaged and repaired on site by de Havilland.
16/03/45	Transferred to 254 Squadron. Sent to Bircham Newton for overhaul.
19/04/45	Delivered to 254 Squadron.
05/07/45	Flying accident category 'Ac'. Re-categorised 'E'.
30/07/45	Struck off charge.

MM424 (39)

12/02/44	10 Maintenance Unit
26/02/44	618 Squadron SD. Coded 'H'.
09/03/44	Flying accident category 'Ac'.
23/05/44	Transferred to 248 Squadron.
17/07/44	Damaged and repaired on site.
16/03/45	Transferred to 254 Squadron and sent to Bircham Newton for overhaul.
16/05/45	Delivered to 254 Squadron.
17/07/45	Damaged Category 'AC'. Repaired on site by 67 Maintenance Unit.
28/08/45	Transferred to 9 Maintenance Unit.
04/11/46	Struck off charge and reduced to produce.

MM425 (48)

02/02/44	A&AEE
26/02/44	Delivered to 618 Squadron SD. Coded 'L'.
23/05/44	Transferred to 248 Squadron.
12/07/44	Damaged and repaired on site.
17/10/44	Damaged and repaired in works, de Havilland, Hatfield.
10/12/44	Flying accident category 'E'
16/12/44	Struck off charge.

NT224 (29)

05/06/44	Delivered to 248 Squadron. Coded 'E1'
17/08/44	Flying accident category 'Ac'. Repaired on site.
06/11/44	Damaged and repaired at Martin Hease.
22/02/45	Damaged and repaired on site by de Havilland, Hatfield.
22/03/45	To Bircham Newton for overhaul.
16/05/45	Transferred to 254 Squadron.
20/08/45	Transferred to 9 Maintenance Unit.
10/11/46	Struck off charge

NT225 (49)

02/06/44	Delivered to 248 Squadron. Coded 'O'.
07/12/44	Shot down by fighter. F/O Cosman/F/O Freedman lost.

PZ251 (5)

13/07/44	Coastal Command Preparation Pool
08/44	Delivered to 248 Squadron. Coded 'I'.
21/10/44	Shot down by flak. F/O Driscoll/F/O Hannant lost.

PZ252 (19)

13/07/44	Coastal Command Preparation Pool
25/08/44	Delivered to 248 Squadron. Coded 'Z1'.
16/03/45	Transferred to 254 Squadron. Coded 'QM-C'.
30/04/45	Damaged and repaired on site by de Havilland.
23/08/45	Transferred to 9 Maintenance Unit.
25/11/46	Struck off charge and reduced to produce.

PZ300 (13)

14/08/44	Coastal Command Preparation Pool
31/08/44	Delivered to 248 Squadron. Coded 'S1'.
24/10/44	Battle damage category 'Ac'. Repaired on site
16/03/45	Transferred to Bircham Newton for overhaul.
21/03/45	Transferred to 254 Squadron. Coded 'QM-A'.
04/05/45	Damaged category 'Ac'. Repaired on site by de Havilland.
24/05/45	Re-categorised Cat 'B' damage. Repaired in works at Martlesham Heath.
03/12/45	Re-categorised as Cat 'E' and struck off charge.

PZ301 (23)

18/08/44	Coastal Command Preparation Pool
31/08/44	Delivered to 248 Squadron. Coded 'T1'.
16/03/45	Transferred to 254 Squadron. Coded 'QM-B'.
05/05/45	Damaged and repaired on site by de Havilland.
03/09/45	Transferred to 9 Maintenance Unit.
31/12/46	Struck off charge and reduced to produce.

PZ346 (8)

05/09/44	Coastal Command Preparation Pool.
28/10/44	Delivered to 248 Squadron. Coded 'Z'.
07/12/44	Shot down by fighter. F/O Wing RCAF/F/Sgt Shield RAAF lost.

PZ467

05/10/44	CRD Hatfield
12/12/44	Transferred to 27 Maintenance Unit.
06/03/45	Transferred to RAF Pershore
09/04/45	Shipped to US Navy at Patuxant River Naval Air Station, Maryland
1946	Sold to Allison Perry. Registered NX66422.
1946	Sold to Marvin Dunlay.
20/09/47	Sold to Maj Jean P Doar. Named 'The Silver Streak'
27/01/48	Swung on landing and undercarriage collapsed. Aircraft scrapped. Merlin engines sold to an individual in Miami for a power boat.

PZ468 (15)

02/11/44	3504 SU
10/11/44	de Havilland
12/12/44	Delivered to 248 Squadron. Coded 'Z'.
14/03/45	Transferred to Bircham Newton for overhaul.
21/03/45	Transferred to 254 Squadron. Coded 'QM-D'.
04/05/45	Damaged category 'Ac'.
20/08/45	Transferred to 9 Maintenance Unit.
26/11/46	Struck off charge and reduced to produce.

PZ469

04/12/44	Delivered to 27 Maintenance Unit.
08/08/45	Transferred to Boscombe Down.
17/10/45	Transferred to 57 Maintenance Unit.
07/08/47	Sold to Linzer and Co for scrap.

PZ470

04/01/45	Delivered to 27 Maintenance Unit.
23/07/46	Struck off charge.

APPENDIX 3

Ammunition expenditure

The following table is for 6pdr ammunition expenditure for the first seven months of 1944.

Date	Tse-tse strength	Operational sorties	Operational expenditure	Expenditure per sortie	Practice expenditure	Total expenditure
Jan '44	1	7	-	-	24	24
Feb '44	2	7	9	1.29	122	131
Mar '44	3	24	231	9.62	126	357
Apr '44	3	26	38	1.46	252	290
May '44	3	17	-	-	258	258
Jun '44	4	44	102	2.3	420	522
Jul '44	4	28	59	2.1	222	281

As can be seen, apart from March, more ammunition was used on target practice than on actual sorties. As only a small number of rounds could be carried the pilots had to make every shot count hence the high practice expenditure.

Mosquito Bibliography

Books

A **Most Secret Squadron** Des Curtis DFC, Skitten Books, Dorset. ISBN 0952524708
A **Separate Little War**. Andrew Bird, Grub Street London. ISBN 1904010431
Bloody Biscay. Chris Goss, Crécy Publishing Ltd. ISBN 0947554629
Dark Sky, Deep Water. Norman Franks. Grub Street, London. ISBN 1902304373.
De Havilland Mosquito. Edward Shacklady. Cerberus. ISBN 1841451088.
Mosquito bomber/fighter-bomber units 1942-45. Martin Bowman, Osprey publishing. ISBN 1855326905
Mosquito in Action part 2. Squadron/Signal 139. ISBN 0897473035
Mosquito Squadrons of the **RAF**. Chaz Bower, Ian Allen Ltd, ISBN 0711014256
Search, Find and Kill. Norman Franks. Grub Street, London. ISBN 1898697353.
The **Strike Wings, Special Anti-Shipping Squadrons 1942-45**. Roy C Nesbit, HMSO Publications, ISBN 0117726877.
The **Wooden Wonder**. Edward Bishop, Airlife Publishing Co. ISBN 0906393043

Official Documents

248 Squadron Operations Record Book	PRO AIR27/1479
248 Squadron Combat Reports	PRO AIR50/312
254 Squadron Operations Record Book	PRO AIR27/
618 Squadron Operations Record Book	PRO AIR27/2130
A&AEE Tse-tse Gunnery Installation	PRO AVIA18/773
The Operations of Mk XVIII Mosquitoes with 6pdr A/U Guns	PRO AIR20/125

Periodicals

Aeroplane
American Aviation Historical Society Journal, Summer 2001.
Flypast
Wings of Fame
Wingspan

Acknowledgments

I would like to thank Andy Bird and his publishers, Grub Street for permission to use details from his book, 'A Separate Little War' and for the use of a number of photos. The same thanks also goes to Des Curtiss DFC for the kind use of extracts from his book 'A Most Secret Squadron' published by Skitten Books. The following people have also helped with the research for this book: A H Hilliard (pilot 618 Squadron SD), Bård Kolltveit, Brian Beattie (pilot 248 Squadron), Brian Thompson, Chris Goss, Colin Jeffrey, Hugh Halliday, Ian Parkins, Kjell Sørensen, Kjetil Åkra, Kyrre Ingebrethsen, Leslie Cook Doughty DFM (pilot 248 Squadron), Mark Felton, Mark L Evans, Norman Malayney, Olve Dybvig, Paul Sedal, Steven Hunter and Tony Williams.

Many thanks to all those individuals who have answered my many questions on the various internet discussion groups/forums:
http://www.warsailors.com/index.html,   http://www.mossie.org/Mosquito.html,
http://disc.server.com/Indices/37919.html,   http://disc.server.com/Indices/104358.html,
www.rafcommands.com/cgi-bin/dcforum/dcboard.cgi,   http://p219.ezboard.com/bwwiiairwaroverthenorth.